50 Japanese Ramen Recipes for Home

By: Kelly Johnson

Table of Contents

- Shoyu Ramen
- Miso Ramen
- Tonkotsu Ramen
- Shio Ramen
- Spicy Tan Tan Ramen
- Vegetarian Ramen
- Chicken Ramen
- Pork Belly Ramen
- Seafood Ramen
- Tsukemen (Dipping Ramen)
- Curry Ramen
- Kimchi Ramen
- Spicy Pork Ramen
- Garlic Ramen
- Sesame Ramen
- Duck Ramen
- Soba Noodle Ramen
- Beef Ramen
- Natto Ramen
- Black Garlic Ramen
- Shrimp Ramen
- Pork Miso Ramen
- Vegan Ramen
- Hakata Ramen
- Hokkaido Ramen
- Nagasaki Champon
- Okinawa Soba
- Tantanmen (Dan Dan Noodles)
- Green Curry Ramen
- Lobster Ramen
- Clam Ramen
- Chicken Paitan Ramen
- Spicy Szechuan Ramen
- Truffle Ramen
- Tsukemen (Cold Dipping Ramen)

- Cheese Ramen
- Tom Yum Ramen
- Mapo Tofu Ramen
- Jjajang Ramen (Black Bean Noodles)
- Tomato Ramen
- Fried Chicken Ramen
- Tempura Ramen
- Uni (Sea Urchin) Ramen
- Gyukotsu Ramen (Beef Bone Ramen)
- Chicken Shio Ramen
- Spicy Shrimp Ramen
- Duck Shoyu Ramen
- Spicy Crab Ramen
- Mushroom Ramen
- Yuzu Ramen

Shoyu Ramen

Ingredients:

For the Broth:

- 8 cups chicken broth (homemade or store-bought)
- 2 cups dashi stock (optional, for added umami)
- 1/4 cup soy sauce
- 2 tablespoons mirin (Japanese sweet rice wine)
- 2 tablespoons sake (Japanese rice wine)
- 1 teaspoon sesame oil

For the Toppings:

- 300g ramen noodles (fresh or dried)
- 2-3 slices of chashu pork (or substitute with roasted pork belly)
- 2 soft-boiled eggs, halved
- 1 sheet of nori (seaweed), cut into halves or quarters
- 1/2 cup bamboo shoots (menma)
- 1/2 cup sliced green onions (scallions)
- Optional: corn kernels, spinach, narutomaki (fish cake), bean sprouts

For Chashu Pork (optional):

- 500g pork belly
- 1/2 cup soy sauce
- 1/2 cup mirin
- 1/2 cup sake
- 1/4 cup sugar
- 2 cups water

Instructions:

1. Prepare the Chashu Pork (if making):

- In a large pot, combine soy sauce, mirin, sake, sugar, and water. Bring to a boil, then reduce to a simmer.
- Add the pork belly and simmer for 1.5 to 2 hours, until tender. Remove from heat and let it cool in the liquid.
- Once cooled, slice the pork belly into thin slices.

2. Prepare the Broth:

- In a large pot, combine chicken broth, dashi stock (if using), soy sauce, mirin, sake, and sesame oil.

- Bring the mixture to a boil, then reduce heat and simmer for about 15-20 minutes to allow the flavors to meld together.

3. Prepare the Toppings:

- Cook the ramen noodles according to package instructions. Drain and rinse briefly under cold water to remove excess starch.
- Soft-boil the eggs: Bring a pot of water to a boil, gently lower the eggs into the water, and cook for 7 minutes. Transfer to an ice bath to stop cooking, then peel and halve them.
- Prepare the bamboo shoots, green onions, nori, and any other desired toppings.

4. Assemble the Ramen:

- Divide the cooked noodles among serving bowls.
- Ladle the hot broth over the noodles.
- Arrange the chashu pork slices, soft-boiled eggs, bamboo shoots, green onions, and nori on top of the noodles.
- Optionally, add other toppings such as corn, spinach, narutomaki, or bean sprouts.

5. Serve:

- Serve hot, garnished with additional green onions if desired.
- Enjoy your homemade Shoyu Ramen with a side of pickled ginger or a sprinkle of shichimi togarashi (Japanese seven spice blend) for added flavor.

Notes:

- **Broth Variations:** Adjust the soy sauce and other seasonings to taste. Some recipes may use kombu (kelp) or bonito flakes instead of dashi stock for a different flavor profile.
- **Noodle Options:** Use fresh ramen noodles for the best texture, but dried noodles can also be used. Follow package instructions for cooking times.
- **Make Ahead:** The broth and chashu pork can be prepared ahead of time and stored separately in the refrigerator. Reheat gently before assembling the ramen.

Enjoy your hearty bowl of Shoyu Ramen, perfect for any time of year!

Miso Ramen

Ingredients:

For the Broth:

- 8 cups chicken or pork broth (homemade or store-bought)
- 1/2 cup white miso paste
- 2 tablespoons soy sauce
- 1 tablespoon sesame oil
- 1 tablespoon mirin (Japanese sweet rice wine)
- 1 teaspoon sugar

For the Toppings:

- 300g ramen noodles (fresh or dried)
- 2-3 slices of chashu pork (or substitute with roasted pork belly)
- 2 soft-boiled eggs, halved
- 1 sheet of nori (seaweed), cut into halves or quarters
- 1/2 cup bamboo shoots (menma)
- 1/2 cup sliced green onions (scallions)
- Optional: corn kernels, spinach, narutomaki (fish cake), bean sprouts

For Chashu Pork (optional):

- 500g pork belly
- 1/2 cup soy sauce
- 1/2 cup mirin
- 1/2 cup sake
- 1/4 cup sugar
- 2 cups water

Instructions:

1. Prepare the Chashu Pork (if making):

- In a large pot, combine soy sauce, mirin, sake, sugar, and water. Bring to a boil, then reduce to a simmer.
- Add the pork belly and simmer for 1.5 to 2 hours, until tender. Remove from heat and let it cool in the liquid.
- Once cooled, slice the pork belly into thin slices.

2. Prepare the Broth:

- In a separate pot, heat the chicken or pork broth over medium heat.
- In a small bowl, whisk together miso paste and a ladle of hot broth until smooth.

- Add the miso mixture, soy sauce, sesame oil, mirin, and sugar to the pot of broth. Stir well to combine.
- Simmer the broth gently for about 10-15 minutes, stirring occasionally, to let the flavors meld together.

3. Prepare the Toppings:

- Cook the ramen noodles according to package instructions. Drain and rinse briefly under cold water to remove excess starch.
- Soft-boil the eggs: Bring a pot of water to a boil, gently lower the eggs into the water, and cook for 7 minutes. Transfer to an ice bath to stop cooking, then peel and halve them.
- Prepare the bamboo shoots, green onions, nori, and any other desired toppings.

4. Assemble the Ramen:

- Divide the cooked noodles among serving bowls.
- Ladle the hot miso broth over the noodles.

5. Add Toppings:

- Arrange the chashu pork slices, soft-boiled eggs, bamboo shoots, green onions, and nori on top of the noodles.
- Optionally, add other toppings such as corn, spinach, narutomaki, or bean sprouts.

6. Serve:

- Serve hot, garnished with additional green onions if desired.
- Enjoy your homemade Miso Ramen with a side of pickled ginger or a sprinkle of sesame seeds for added flavor.

Notes:

- **Miso Paste:** There are different types of miso paste (white, red, yellow) with varying levels of sweetness and saltiness. Adjust the amount according to your preference and the type of miso you have.
- **Noodle Options:** Use fresh ramen noodles for the best texture, but dried noodles can also be used. Follow package instructions for cooking times.
- **Make Ahead:** The broth and chashu pork can be prepared ahead of time and stored separately in the refrigerator. Reheat gently before assembling the ramen.

Enjoy your comforting bowl of Miso Ramen, perfect for warming up on a chilly day!

Tonkotsu Ramen

Ingredients:

For the Tonkotsu Broth:

- 2-3 lbs pork bones (such as neck bones, trotters, or knuckles)
- 1 onion, peeled and halved
- 1 head of garlic, halved crosswise
- 1 knob of ginger, sliced
- 1 leek, chopped (optional)
- 1 tablespoon vegetable oil
- Water, enough to cover the bones (about 12 cups)
- Salt, to taste

For the Tare (Seasoning Sauce):

- 1/2 cup soy sauce
- 1/4 cup mirin (Japanese sweet rice wine)
- 1/4 cup sake (Japanese rice wine)

For the Ramen:

- 300g fresh ramen noodles
- Chashu pork slices (from the broth recipe below)
- Soft-boiled eggs, halved
- Menma (bamboo shoots)
- Nori (seaweed sheets), cut into halves or quarters
- Green onions (scallions), thinly sliced
- Optional: corn kernels, spinach, narutomaki (fish cake), bean sprouts

Instructions:

1. Prepare the Tonkotsu Broth:

- Rinse the pork bones under cold water to remove any blood or impurities.
- In a large pot or pressure cooker, heat vegetable oil over medium-high heat. Add the pork bones and sear them until browned on all sides.
- Add onion, garlic, ginger, leek (if using), and enough water to cover the bones (about 12 cups).
- Bring to a boil, then reduce heat to low and simmer gently for at least 8 hours (or up to 24 hours for richer flavor), skimming any scum that rises to the surface.
- Alternatively, use a pressure cooker for 3-4 hours to achieve similar results.
- Strain the broth through a fine mesh sieve or cheesecloth. Discard solids. Season with salt to taste.

2. Prepare the Chashu Pork:

- While the broth is simmering, prepare the chashu pork. Use pork belly or pork shoulder.
- In a pot, combine soy sauce, mirin, sake, sugar, and water. Bring to a boil, then reduce to a simmer.
- Add the pork and simmer for 1.5 to 2 hours until tender. Let cool in the liquid, then slice thinly.

3. Prepare the Tare (Seasoning Sauce):

- In a small saucepan, combine soy sauce, mirin, and sake. Bring to a boil, then simmer for 5-10 minutes until slightly reduced. Set aside.

4. Prepare Ramen Toppings:

- Soft-boil eggs: Bring a pot of water to a boil, gently lower eggs into the water, and cook for 7 minutes. Transfer to an ice bath, peel, and halve them.
- Prepare other toppings like menma, nori, green onions, and any additional toppings of your choice.

5. Cook Ramen Noodles:

- Cook fresh ramen noodles according to package instructions. Drain and rinse briefly under cold water to remove excess starch.

6. Assemble Tonkotsu Ramen:

- Divide the cooked noodles among serving bowls.
- Ladle the hot tonkotsu broth over the noodles.
- Add a spoonful of tare (seasoning sauce) to each bowl, adjusting to taste.
- Arrange chashu pork slices, soft-boiled eggs, menma, nori, green onions, and other toppings on top of the noodles.

7. Serve:

- Serve hot, optionally garnished with a sprinkle of sesame seeds or a drizzle of sesame oil.
- Enjoy your homemade Tonkotsu Ramen!

Notes:

- **Broth:** Traditional tonkotsu broth is rich and creamy due to the gelatin released from long-simmered pork bones. Take your time to simmer the broth for the best flavor.
- **Noodles:** Fresh ramen noodles are preferable for authenticity, but dried noodles can also be used. Adjust cooking times accordingly.

- **Make Ahead:** Broth and chashu pork can be made ahead of time and stored in the refrigerator. Reheat gently before serving.

Enjoy the comforting and flavorful bowl of Tonkotsu Ramen, a favorite among ramen enthusiasts!

Shio Ramen

Ingredients:

For the Broth:

- 8 cups chicken or pork broth (homemade or store-bought)
- 2 cups dashi stock (optional, for added depth)
- 2 tablespoons soy sauce
- 2 tablespoons sake (Japanese rice wine)
- 1 tablespoon mirin (Japanese sweet rice wine)
- 1 teaspoon salt (adjust to taste)
- 1 teaspoon sesame oil

For the Toppings:

- 300g ramen noodles (fresh or dried)
- Chashu pork slices (from the Tonkotsu Ramen recipe or substitute with roasted pork belly)
- Soft-boiled eggs, halved
- Bamboo shoots (menma)
- Nori (seaweed sheets), cut into halves or quarters
- Green onions (scallions), thinly sliced
- Optional: corn kernels, spinach, narutomaki (fish cake), bean sprouts

Instructions:

1. Prepare the Broth:

- In a large pot, combine chicken or pork broth and dashi stock (if using).
- Add soy sauce, sake, mirin, salt, and sesame oil. Stir well to combine.
- Bring the mixture to a boil, then reduce heat to low and simmer gently for about 15-20 minutes to allow the flavors to meld together.

2. Prepare the Ramen Toppings:

- Cook the ramen noodles according to package instructions. Drain and rinse briefly under cold water to remove excess starch.
- Soft-boil the eggs: Bring a pot of water to a boil, gently lower the eggs into the water, and cook for 7 minutes. Transfer to an ice bath to stop cooking, then peel and halve them.
- Prepare other toppings like chashu pork slices, bamboo shoots (menma), nori (seaweed sheets), green onions (scallions), and any additional toppings of your choice.

3. Assemble the Shio Ramen:

- Divide the cooked ramen noodles among serving bowls.

- Ladle the hot shio broth over the noodles. Adjust the saltiness of the broth according to your taste.
- Arrange chashu pork slices, soft-boiled eggs, bamboo shoots (menma), nori (seaweed sheets), green onions (scallions), and any other toppings on top of the noodles.

4. Serve:

- Serve hot, optionally garnished with a sprinkle of sesame seeds or a drizzle of sesame oil.
- Enjoy your homemade Shio Ramen, a light and comforting noodle soup!

Notes:

- **Broth Variation:** Shio Ramen traditionally has a light and clear broth. Adjust the saltiness by adding more or less salt according to your preference.
- **Noodles:** Fresh ramen noodles are ideal for the best texture, but dried noodles can also be used. Follow the package instructions for cooking times.
- **Make Ahead:** Both the broth and toppings can be prepared ahead of time and stored separately in the refrigerator. Reheat gently before serving.

Enjoy your bowl of Shio Ramen with its delicate flavors and satisfying noodles!

Spicy Tan Tan Ramen

Ingredients:

For the Spicy Tan Tan Soup Base:

- 2 tablespoons sesame paste (tahini)
- 2 tablespoons soy sauce
- 1 tablespoon miso paste (white or red)
- 1 tablespoon doubanjiang (spicy bean paste)
- 1 tablespoon chili oil (adjust to taste)
- 1 teaspoon sesame oil
- 1 teaspoon sugar
- 4 cups chicken or vegetable broth
- 2 cloves garlic, minced
- 1 teaspoon grated ginger

For the Ramen:

- 300g ramen noodles (fresh or dried)
- 200g ground pork or chicken
- 2 tablespoons soy sauce
- 1 tablespoon sake (Japanese rice wine)
- 1 tablespoon mirin (Japanese sweet rice wine)
- 1 teaspoon sugar
- 2 cups baby spinach or bok choy, chopped
- 2 soft-boiled eggs, halved
- 1 sheet nori (seaweed), cut into halves or quarters
- 2-3 green onions (scallions), thinly sliced
- Optional: crushed peanuts, sesame seeds for garnish

Instructions:

1. Prepare the Spicy Tan Tan Soup Base:

- In a mixing bowl, combine sesame paste (tahini), soy sauce, miso paste, doubanjiang (spicy bean paste), chili oil, sesame oil, and sugar. Mix until well combined into a smooth paste.
- In a large pot, heat a tablespoon of vegetable oil over medium heat. Add minced garlic and grated ginger, sauté for about 1 minute until fragrant.
- Add the spicy paste mixture to the pot and stir-fry for another 1-2 minutes until aromatic.
- Pour in chicken or vegetable broth, stirring continuously to incorporate the spicy paste into the broth. Bring to a simmer and let it cook gently for 10-15 minutes to meld the flavors together.

2. Prepare the Ramen Toppings:

- Cook the ramen noodles according to package instructions. Drain and rinse briefly under cold water to remove excess starch.
- In a separate skillet, heat a tablespoon of vegetable oil over medium-high heat. Add ground pork or chicken, breaking it up with a spatula.
- Cook until browned and cooked through. Add soy sauce, sake, mirin, and sugar. Cook for another 2-3 minutes until the meat is coated and the sauce is slightly thickened.
- Add chopped spinach or bok choy to the skillet and stir-fry until wilted. Remove from heat.

3. Assemble Spicy Tan Tan Ramen:

- Divide the cooked ramen noodles among serving bowls.
- Ladle the hot spicy tan tan soup base over the noodles.
- Top each bowl with a portion of the ground meat and vegetable mixture.
- Garnish with soft-boiled eggs, nori (seaweed), green onions (scallions), and any additional toppings like crushed peanuts or sesame seeds.

4. Serve:

- Serve hot, optionally garnished with a sprinkle of sesame seeds or a drizzle of extra chili oil for extra heat.
- Enjoy your homemade Spicy Tan Tan Ramen, a delightful fusion of Japanese and Sichuan flavors!

Notes:

- **Spice Level:** Adjust the amount of chili oil and doubanjiang according to your preference for spiciness.
- **Noodles:** Fresh ramen noodles are recommended for the best texture, but dried noodles can also be used. Follow the package instructions for cooking times.
- **Make Ahead:** The spicy tan tan soup base can be made ahead of time and stored in the refrigerator. Reheat gently before serving.

Enjoy the bold and spicy flavors of Spicy Tan Tan Ramen with its satisfying noodle soup base!

Vegetarian Ramen

Ingredients:

For the Vegetarian Ramen Broth:

- 8 cups vegetable broth (homemade or store-bought)
- 2 cups dashi stock (optional, for added depth)
- 2 tablespoons soy sauce (or tamari for gluten-free)
- 1 tablespoon miso paste (white or red)
- 1 tablespoon mirin (Japanese sweet rice wine)
- 1 tablespoon sesame oil
- 1 teaspoon grated ginger
- 2 cloves garlic, minced
- 1 teaspoon sugar
- Salt and pepper, to taste

For the Ramen:

- 300g ramen noodles (fresh or dried)
- Tofu, sliced and pan-fried or baked
- Soft-boiled eggs (optional, omit for vegan version)
- Bamboo shoots (menma)
- Baby spinach or bok choy, lightly blanched
- Nori (seaweed sheets), cut into halves or quarters
- Green onions (scallions), thinly sliced
- Shiitake mushrooms, sliced and sautéed
- Corn kernels (optional)
- Bean sprouts (optional)
- Sesame seeds, for garnish
- Chili oil or sesame oil, for drizzling (optional)

Instructions:

1. Prepare the Vegetarian Ramen Broth:

- In a large pot, combine vegetable broth and dashi stock (if using).
- Add soy sauce, miso paste, mirin, sesame oil, grated ginger, minced garlic, and sugar. Stir well to combine.
- Bring the mixture to a boil, then reduce heat to low and simmer gently for about 15-20 minutes to allow the flavors to meld together.
- Season with salt and pepper to taste.

2. Prepare the Ramen Toppings:

- Cook the ramen noodles according to package instructions. Drain and rinse briefly under cold water to remove excess starch.
- Prepare tofu: Slice tofu into cubes or rectangles, and pan-fry or bake until golden and crispy on the outside. Season with soy sauce or tamari if desired.
- Soft-boil eggs (if using): Bring a pot of water to a boil, gently lower eggs into the water, and cook for 7 minutes. Transfer to an ice bath, peel, and halve them.
- Lightly blanch baby spinach or bok choy in boiling water for 1-2 minutes until tender-crisp. Drain and set aside.
- Sauté shiitake mushrooms in a bit of oil until softened and lightly browned.

3. Assemble Vegetarian Ramen:

- Divide the cooked ramen noodles among serving bowls.
- Ladle the hot vegetarian ramen broth over the noodles.
- Arrange tofu slices, soft-boiled eggs (if using), bamboo shoots (menma), blanched greens, sautéed mushrooms, nori (seaweed sheets), and green onions (scallions) on top of the noodles.
- Optionally, add corn kernels, bean sprouts, sesame seeds, and a drizzle of chili oil or sesame oil for extra flavor.

4. Serve:

- Serve hot, optionally garnished with additional green onions or sesame seeds.
- Enjoy your homemade Vegetarian Ramen, a comforting and satisfying noodle soup!

Notes:

- **Broth Variation:** Adjust the seasoning of the broth according to your preference. You can also add other umami-rich ingredients like dried shiitake mushrooms or kombu (kelp) for more depth of flavor.
- **Noodles:** Fresh ramen noodles are recommended for the best texture, but dried noodles can also be used. Follow the package instructions for cooking times.
- **Make Ahead:** The broth and toppings can be prepared ahead of time and stored separately in the refrigerator. Reheat gently before assembling the ramen.

This Vegetarian Ramen recipe allows you to enjoy a flavorful and hearty bowl of noodles, packed with wholesome vegetables and plant-based proteins!

Chicken Ramen

Ingredients:

For the Chicken Broth:

- 8 cups chicken broth (homemade or store-bought)
- 2 cups dashi stock (optional, for added umami)
- 2 tablespoons soy sauce
- 1 tablespoon mirin (Japanese sweet rice wine)
- 1 teaspoon sesame oil
- Salt, to taste

For the Ramen:

- 300g ramen noodles (fresh or dried)
- 2 boneless, skinless chicken breasts
- 2 soft-boiled eggs, halved
- 2 sheets nori (seaweed), cut into halves or quarters
- 1 cup bamboo shoots (menma)
- 2-3 green onions (scallions), thinly sliced
- 1 tablespoon sesame seeds, for garnish
- Optional: corn kernels, spinach, narutomaki (fish cake), bean sprouts

Instructions:

1. Prepare the Chicken Broth:

- In a large pot, combine chicken broth and dashi stock (if using).
- Add soy sauce, mirin, sesame oil, and salt. Stir well to combine.
- Bring the mixture to a boil over medium-high heat, then reduce heat to low and simmer for about 15-20 minutes to allow the flavors to meld together.

2. Prepare the Chicken:

- Bring a pot of water to a boil. Add the chicken breasts and cook for 10-12 minutes, or until cooked through.
- Remove the chicken from the pot and let it rest for a few minutes before slicing thinly.

3. Prepare the Ramen Toppings:

- Cook the ramen noodles according to package instructions. Drain and rinse briefly under cold water to remove excess starch.
- Soft-boil the eggs: Bring a pot of water to a boil, gently lower the eggs into the water, and cook for 7 minutes. Transfer to an ice bath to stop cooking, then peel and halve them.

- Prepare other toppings like bamboo shoots (menma), nori (seaweed sheets), green onions (scallions), and any additional toppings of your choice.

4. Assemble Chicken Ramen:

- Divide the cooked ramen noodles among serving bowls.
- Ladle the hot chicken broth over the noodles.
- Arrange slices of cooked chicken breast, soft-boiled eggs, bamboo shoots (menma), nori (seaweed sheets), and green onions (scallions) on top of the noodles.
- Optionally, add corn kernels, spinach, narutomaki (fish cake), bean sprouts, or any other toppings you prefer.

5. Serve:

- Garnish with sesame seeds and a drizzle of sesame oil if desired.
- Serve hot and enjoy your homemade Chicken Ramen!

Notes:

- **Broth Variation:** For a richer flavor, you can add chicken bones (such as wings or thighs) to the broth and simmer for longer to extract more depth.
- **Noodles:** Fresh ramen noodles are preferred for their texture, but dried noodles work well too. Follow package instructions for cooking times.
- **Make Ahead:** The broth can be prepared ahead of time and stored in the refrigerator. Reheat gently before assembling the ramen.

This Chicken Ramen recipe is perfect for a comforting meal, showcasing the delicate flavors of the broth and the satisfying textures of the toppings. Enjoy!

Pork Belly Ramen

Ingredients:

For the Pork Belly:

- 1 lb pork belly
- 2 tablespoons soy sauce
- 2 tablespoons mirin (Japanese sweet rice wine)
- 1 tablespoon sake (Japanese rice wine)
- 1 tablespoon sugar
- 2 cloves garlic, minced
- 1-inch piece ginger, sliced
- 2 green onions (scallions), chopped

For the Ramen Broth:

- 8 cups chicken broth (homemade or store-bought)
- 2 cups dashi stock (optional, for added umami)
- 2 tablespoons soy sauce
- 1 tablespoon mirin
- 1 tablespoon sesame oil
- Salt, to taste

For the Ramen:

- 300g ramen noodles (fresh or dried)
- Soft-boiled eggs, halved
- Bamboo shoots (menma)
- Nori (seaweed sheets), cut into halves or quarters
- Green onions (scallions), thinly sliced
- Optional: corn kernels, spinach, narutomaki (fish cake), bean sprouts

Instructions:

1. Prepare the Pork Belly:

- In a pot of boiling water, blanch the pork belly for 3-4 minutes to remove impurities. Remove from water and pat dry with paper towels.
- In a bowl, combine soy sauce, mirin, sake, sugar, minced garlic, sliced ginger, and chopped green onions.
- Place the pork belly in a resealable bag or shallow dish, and pour the marinade over it. Marinate in the refrigerator for at least 2 hours, or overnight for best results.

- Preheat the oven to 375°F (190°C). Remove the pork belly from the marinade (reserve the marinade) and place it on a baking sheet lined with foil. Bake for 40-45 minutes, until the pork belly is tender and caramelized. Let it cool slightly, then slice thinly.

2. Prepare the Ramen Broth:

- In a large pot, combine chicken broth and dashi stock (if using).
- Add soy sauce, mirin, sesame oil, and salt. Stir well to combine.
- Bring the mixture to a boil over medium-high heat, then reduce heat to low and simmer for about 15-20 minutes to allow the flavors to meld together.

3. Prepare the Ramen Toppings:

- Cook the ramen noodles according to package instructions. Drain and rinse briefly under cold water to remove excess starch.
- Soft-boil the eggs: Bring a pot of water to a boil, gently lower eggs into the water, and cook for 7 minutes. Transfer to an ice bath to stop cooking, then peel and halve them.
- Prepare other toppings like bamboo shoots (menma), nori (seaweed sheets), green onions (scallions), and any additional toppings of your choice.

4. Assemble Pork Belly Ramen:

- Divide the cooked ramen noodles among serving bowls.
- Ladle the hot ramen broth over the noodles.
- Arrange slices of cooked pork belly, soft-boiled eggs, bamboo shoots (menma), nori (seaweed sheets), and green onions (scallions) on top of the noodles.
- Optionally, add corn kernels, spinach, narutomaki (fish cake), bean sprouts, or any other toppings you prefer.

5. Serve:

- Serve hot and enjoy your homemade Pork Belly Ramen!

Notes:

- **Broth Variation:** For a richer flavor, you can add pork bones (such as neck bones or trotters) to the broth and simmer for longer to extract more depth.
- **Noodles:** Fresh ramen noodles are recommended for their texture, but dried noodles work well too. Follow package instructions for cooking times.
- **Make Ahead:** The pork belly can be marinated and baked ahead of time. Store leftovers in the refrigerator and reheat gently before serving.

This Pork Belly Ramen recipe will delight your taste buds with its rich broth and tender slices of pork belly, creating a satisfying bowl of comfort. Enjoy!

Seafood Ramen

Ingredients:

For the Seafood Broth:

- 8 cups seafood broth (homemade or store-bought)
- 2 cups dashi stock (optional, for added depth)
- 2 tablespoons soy sauce
- 1 tablespoon mirin (Japanese sweet rice wine)
- 1 tablespoon sake (Japanese rice wine)
- 1 tablespoon sesame oil
- 1 tablespoon miso paste (white or red)
- Salt and pepper, to taste

For the Ramen:

- 300g ramen noodles (fresh or dried)
- Assorted seafood such as shrimp, squid, mussels, and/or scallops (cleaned and deveined)
- 2 soft-boiled eggs, halved
- Bamboo shoots (menma)
- Nori (seaweed sheets), cut into halves or quarters
- Green onions (scallions), thinly sliced
- Optional: corn kernels, spinach, narutomaki (fish cake), bean sprouts

Instructions:

1. Prepare the Seafood Broth:

- In a large pot, combine seafood broth and dashi stock (if using).
- Add soy sauce, mirin, sake, sesame oil, and miso paste. Stir well to combine.
- Bring the mixture to a boil over medium-high heat, then reduce heat to low and simmer for about 15-20 minutes to allow the flavors to meld together.
- Season with salt and pepper to taste.

2. Prepare the Ramen Toppings:

- Cook the ramen noodles according to package instructions. Drain and rinse briefly under cold water to remove excess starch.
- Prepare assorted seafood: If using shrimp, squid, or scallops, cook them briefly in a separate skillet until just cooked through. Season lightly with salt and pepper.
- Soft-boil the eggs: Bring a pot of water to a boil, gently lower eggs into the water, and cook for 7 minutes. Transfer to an ice bath to stop cooking, then peel and halve them.

- Prepare other toppings like bamboo shoots (menma), nori (seaweed sheets), green onions (scallions), and any additional toppings of your choice.

3. Assemble Seafood Ramen:

- Divide the cooked ramen noodles among serving bowls.
- Ladle the hot seafood broth over the noodles.
- Arrange cooked seafood, soft-boiled eggs, bamboo shoots (menma), nori (seaweed sheets), and green onions (scallions) on top of the noodles.
- Optionally, add corn kernels, spinach, narutomaki (fish cake), bean sprouts, or any other toppings you prefer.

4. Serve:

- Serve hot and enjoy your homemade Seafood Ramen!

Notes:

- **Seafood Variation:** You can customize the seafood according to your preferences or what's available fresh. Feel free to add clams, lobster, or any other seafood you enjoy.
- **Broth Variation:** For a richer flavor, you can add seafood shells (like shrimp shells) to the broth and simmer for longer to extract more depth.
- **Noodles:** Fresh ramen noodles are recommended for their texture, but dried noodles work well too. Follow package instructions for cooking times.
- **Make Ahead:** The seafood broth can be prepared ahead of time and stored in the refrigerator. Reheat gently before assembling the ramen.

This Seafood Ramen recipe will bring the flavors of the ocean to your table, creating a delicious and comforting bowl of noodle soup. Enjoy the delightful combination of seafood and savory broth!

Tsukemen (Dipping Ramen)

Ingredients:

For the Dipping Broth:

- 4 cups chicken or pork broth (homemade or store-bought)
- 2 cups dashi stock (optional, for added depth)
- 1/4 cup soy sauce
- 2 tablespoons mirin (Japanese sweet rice wine)
- 1 tablespoon sake (Japanese rice wine)
- 1 tablespoon sugar
- 1 teaspoon sesame oil
- 2 cloves garlic, minced
- 1-inch piece ginger, sliced
- 1 green onion (scallion), chopped
- 1 tablespoon bonito flakes (optional, for extra umami)

For the Ramen:

- 300g ramen noodles (fresh or dried)
- Chashu pork slices (from your preferred ramen recipe or substitute with roasted pork belly)
- Soft-boiled eggs, halved
- Bamboo shoots (menma)
- Nori (seaweed sheets), cut into halves or quarters
- Green onions (scallions), thinly sliced
- Optional: spinach, narutomaki (fish cake), bean sprouts

Instructions:

1. Prepare the Dipping Broth:

- In a large pot, combine chicken or pork broth and dashi stock (if using).
- Add soy sauce, mirin, sake, sugar, sesame oil, minced garlic, sliced ginger, green onion, and bonito flakes (if using).
- Bring the mixture to a boil over medium-high heat, then reduce heat to low and simmer for about 15-20 minutes to allow the flavors to meld together.
- Strain the broth through a fine mesh sieve to remove solids. Keep the broth hot while preparing the noodles.

2. Prepare the Ramen Toppings:

- Cook the ramen noodles according to package instructions. Drain and rinse briefly under cold water to remove excess starch.

- Slice chashu pork into thin slices.
- Soft-boil the eggs: Bring a pot of water to a boil, gently lower eggs into the water, and cook for 7 minutes. Transfer to an ice bath to stop cooking, then peel and halve them.
- Prepare other toppings like bamboo shoots (menma), nori (seaweed sheets), green onions (scallions), and any additional toppings of your choice.

3. Assemble Tsukemen (Dipping Ramen):

- Divide the cooked ramen noodles among serving bowls or onto a large plate.
- Serve the hot dipping broth in separate bowls or a large shallow dish alongside the noodles.
- Arrange slices of chashu pork, soft-boiled eggs, bamboo shoots (menma), nori (seaweed sheets), green onions (scallions), and any other toppings you prepared around or on top of the noodles.

4. Serve:

- To eat, take a portion of noodles with chopsticks and dip them into the hot dipping broth. Enjoy the noodles and toppings with the flavorful broth.
- Optionally, sprinkle with sesame seeds or drizzle with a bit of chili oil for extra flavor.

Notes:

- **Broth Variation:** Adjust the seasoning of the dipping broth according to your preference. You can also add more soy sauce or mirin for a sweeter or saltier taste.
- **Noodles:** Fresh ramen noodles are recommended for their texture, but dried noodles can be used. Follow the package instructions for cooking times.
- **Make Ahead:** The dipping broth can be prepared ahead of time and stored in the refrigerator. Reheat gently before serving.

Tsukemen is a delicious way to enjoy ramen, with the noodles and toppings dipped into a rich and flavorful broth, offering a unique and satisfying dining experience.

Curry Ramen

Ingredients:

For the Curry Broth:

- 2 tablespoons vegetable oil
- 1 onion, finely chopped
- 2 cloves garlic, minced
- 1 tablespoon ginger, grated
- 2 tablespoons curry powder (Japanese curry powder recommended)
- 1 tablespoon tomato paste
- 4 cups vegetable or chicken broth
- 1 can (14 oz) coconut milk
- 2 tablespoons soy sauce
- 1 tablespoon mirin (Japanese sweet rice wine)
- 1 tablespoon brown sugar
- Salt and pepper, to taste

For the Ramen:

- 300g ramen noodles (fresh or dried)
- 1 cup mushrooms, sliced (shiitake or cremini recommended)
- 1 cup spinach or baby bok choy, chopped
- 1 block tofu, cut into cubes and pan-fried (optional)
- Soft-boiled eggs, halved
- Green onions (scallions), thinly sliced
- Nori (seaweed sheets), cut into halves or quarters
- Sesame seeds, for garnish
- Optional: corn kernels, bean sprouts, bamboo shoots (menma)

Instructions:

1. Prepare the Curry Broth:

- Heat vegetable oil in a large pot over medium heat. Add chopped onion and cook until softened, about 5-7 minutes.
- Add minced garlic, grated ginger, and curry powder. Cook for another 1-2 minutes until fragrant.
- Stir in tomato paste and cook for 1 minute.
- Pour in vegetable or chicken broth, coconut milk, soy sauce, mirin, and brown sugar. Bring to a simmer and cook for 15-20 minutes, stirring occasionally.

- Season with salt and pepper to taste. Adjust the curry flavor by adding more curry powder if desired.

2. Prepare the Ramen Toppings:

- Cook the ramen noodles according to package instructions. Drain and rinse briefly under cold water to remove excess starch.
- In a separate pan, sauté sliced mushrooms until softened. Set aside.
- If using tofu, cut into cubes and pan-fry until golden brown on all sides.
- Soft-boil the eggs: Bring a pot of water to a boil, gently lower eggs into the water, and cook for 7 minutes. Transfer to an ice bath to stop cooking, then peel and halve them.
- Prepare other toppings like chopped spinach or baby bok choy, green onions (scallions), nori (seaweed sheets), sesame seeds, and any additional toppings of your choice.

3. Assemble Curry Ramen:

- Divide the cooked ramen noodles among serving bowls.
- Ladle the hot curry broth over the noodles.
- Arrange sautéed mushrooms, tofu cubes (if using), soft-boiled eggs, chopped spinach or bok choy, green onions (scallions), nori (seaweed sheets), and any other toppings you prepared on top of the noodles.
- Optionally, add corn kernels, bean sprouts, bamboo shoots (menma), or additional garnishes like a sprinkle of sesame seeds.

4. Serve:

- Serve hot and enjoy your homemade Curry Ramen!

Notes:

- **Curry Powder:** Japanese curry powder typically includes a blend of spices like turmeric, cumin, coriander, and fenugreek. Adjust the amount based on your preference for spice and flavor intensity.
- **Broth Variation:** You can customize the curry broth by adding more coconut milk for creaminess or adjusting the sweetness with more mirin or brown sugar.
- **Noodles:** Fresh ramen noodles are recommended for their texture, but dried noodles can also be used. Follow package instructions for cooking times.
- **Make Ahead:** The curry broth can be made ahead of time and stored in the refrigerator. Reheat gently before serving.

This Curry Ramen recipe combines the comforting flavors of curry with the satisfying elements of ramen, creating a hearty and flavorful dish that's perfect for any occasion. Enjoy!

Kimchi Ramen

Ingredients:

For the Broth:

- 4 cups chicken or vegetable broth (homemade or store-bought)
- 2 cups water
- 1 cup kimchi, chopped
- 2 tablespoons gochujang (Korean red chili paste)
- 2 tablespoons soy sauce
- 1 tablespoon sesame oil
- 1 tablespoon rice vinegar
- 1 tablespoon mirin (Japanese sweet rice wine)
- 2 cloves garlic, minced
- 1-inch piece ginger, grated
- Salt and pepper, to taste

For the Ramen:

- 300g ramen noodles (fresh or dried)
- 1 cup mushrooms, sliced (shiitake or cremini recommended)
- 1 cup spinach or baby bok choy, chopped
- 1 block tofu, cut into cubes and pan-fried (optional)
- Soft-boiled eggs, halved
- Green onions (scallions), thinly sliced
- Nori (seaweed sheets), cut into halves or quarters
- Sesame seeds, for garnish
- Optional: corn kernels, bean sprouts, bamboo shoots (menma)

Instructions:

1. Prepare the Kimchi Broth:

- In a large pot, combine chicken or vegetable broth and water.
- Add chopped kimchi, gochujang, soy sauce, sesame oil, rice vinegar, mirin, minced garlic, and grated ginger. Stir well to combine.
- Bring the mixture to a boil over medium-high heat. Once boiling, reduce the heat to low and let it simmer for about 15-20 minutes to allow the flavors to meld together.
- Taste and adjust seasoning with salt and pepper as needed. Keep the broth hot while preparing the noodles and toppings.

2. Prepare the Ramen Toppings:

- Cook the ramen noodles according to package instructions. Drain and rinse briefly under cold water to remove excess starch.
- In a separate pan, sauté sliced mushrooms until softened. Set aside.
- If using tofu, cut into cubes and pan-fry until golden brown on all sides.
- Soft-boil the eggs: Bring a pot of water to a boil, gently lower eggs into the water, and cook for 7 minutes. Transfer to an ice bath to stop cooking, then peel and halve them.
- Prepare other toppings like chopped spinach or baby bok choy, green onions (scallions), nori (seaweed sheets), sesame seeds, and any additional toppings of your choice.

3. Assemble Kimchi Ramen:

- Divide the cooked ramen noodles among serving bowls.
- Ladle the hot kimchi broth over the noodles.
- Arrange sautéed mushrooms, tofu cubes (if using), soft-boiled eggs, chopped spinach or bok choy, green onions (scallions), nori (seaweed sheets), and any other toppings you prepared on top of the noodles.
- Optionally, add corn kernels, bean sprouts, bamboo shoots (menma), or additional garnishes like a sprinkle of sesame seeds.

4. Serve:

- Serve hot and enjoy your homemade Kimchi Ramen!

Notes:

- **Kimchi:** The quality and spiciness of kimchi can vary, so adjust the amount according to your preference. You can also add kimchi juice for extra tanginess.
- **Broth Variation:** For a richer broth, you can add a dash of fish sauce or chicken bouillon powder. Adjust the spiciness with more gochujang if desired.
- **Noodles:** Fresh ramen noodles are recommended for their texture, but dried noodles can be used. Follow package instructions for cooking times.
- **Make Ahead:** The kimchi broth can be made ahead of time and stored in the refrigerator. Reheat gently before serving.

Kimchi Ramen is a flavorful and comforting dish that combines the bold flavors of kimchi with the savory elements of ramen, making it a satisfying meal for any occasion. Enjoy the spicy kick and umami goodness in each bowl!

Spicy Pork Ramen

Ingredients:

For the Spicy Pork Broth:

- 4 cups chicken or pork broth (homemade or store-bought)
- 2 cups water
- 2 tablespoons miso paste (white or red)
- 2 tablespoons soy sauce
- 1 tablespoon sesame oil
- 1 tablespoon chili paste or chili oil (adjust to taste)
- 2 cloves garlic, minced
- 1-inch piece ginger, grated
- 1 tablespoon rice vinegar
- 1 tablespoon mirin (Japanese sweet rice wine)
- Salt and pepper, to taste

For the Pork:

- 1 lb pork loin or pork shoulder, thinly sliced
- 2 tablespoons soy sauce
- 1 tablespoon mirin
- 1 tablespoon sesame oil
- 1 tablespoon cornstarch

For the Ramen:

- 300g ramen noodles (fresh or dried)
- Soft-boiled eggs, halved
- Green onions (scallions), thinly sliced
- Nori (seaweed sheets), cut into halves or quarters
- Bamboo shoots (menma)
- Optional: spinach, bean sprouts, corn kernels

Instructions:

1. Prepare the Spicy Pork Broth:

- In a large pot, combine chicken or pork broth and water.
- Add miso paste, soy sauce, sesame oil, chili paste or chili oil, minced garlic, grated ginger, rice vinegar, and mirin. Stir well to combine.
- Bring the mixture to a boil over medium-high heat. Reduce heat to low and let it simmer for about 15-20 minutes to allow the flavors to meld together.

- Season with salt and pepper to taste. Keep the broth hot while preparing the noodles and toppings.

2. Prepare the Pork:

- In a bowl, combine soy sauce, mirin, sesame oil, and cornstarch.
- Add thinly sliced pork and marinate for about 15-30 minutes.
- Heat a skillet or frying pan over medium-high heat. Cook the pork slices for 2-3 minutes per side, or until cooked through and nicely browned. Set aside.

3. Prepare the Ramen Toppings:

- Cook the ramen noodles according to package instructions. Drain and rinse briefly under cold water to remove excess starch.
- Soft-boil the eggs: Bring a pot of water to a boil, gently lower eggs into the water, and cook for 7 minutes. Transfer to an ice bath to stop cooking, then peel and halve them.
- Prepare other toppings like thinly sliced green onions (scallions), nori (seaweed sheets), bamboo shoots (menma), and any additional toppings you prefer.

4. Assemble Spicy Pork Ramen:

- Divide the cooked ramen noodles among serving bowls.
- Ladle the hot spicy pork broth over the noodles.
- Arrange cooked pork slices, soft-boiled eggs, green onions (scallions), nori (seaweed sheets), bamboo shoots (menma), and any other toppings you prepared on top of the noodles.
- Optionally, add spinach, bean sprouts, corn kernels, or additional garnishes of your choice.

5. Serve:

- Serve hot and enjoy your homemade Spicy Pork Ramen!

Notes:

- **Spiciness:** Adjust the amount of chili paste or chili oil according to your preference for spiciness. You can start with a smaller amount and add more gradually to reach your desired level of heat.
- **Broth Variation:** For a richer flavor, you can add chicken or pork bones (such as neck bones or ribs) to the broth and simmer for longer to extract more depth.
- **Noodles:** Fresh ramen noodles are recommended for their texture, but dried noodles can be used. Follow package instructions for cooking times.
- **Make Ahead:** The spicy pork broth can be prepared ahead of time and stored in the refrigerator. Reheat gently before serving.

This Spicy Pork Ramen recipe offers a comforting bowl of noodles with a kick of spice, perfect for warming up on chilly days or satisfying your craving for bold flavors. Enjoy the hearty goodness of this homemade ramen!

Garlic Ramen

Ingredients:

For the Garlic Broth:

- 4 cups chicken or vegetable broth (homemade or store-bought)
- 2 cups water
- 8-10 cloves garlic, minced
- 2 tablespoons soy sauce
- 1 tablespoon sesame oil
- 1 tablespoon mirin (Japanese sweet rice wine)
- 1 tablespoon rice vinegar
- 1 teaspoon sugar
- Salt and pepper, to taste

For the Ramen:

- 300g ramen noodles (fresh or dried)
- Chashu pork slices or roasted pork belly (optional)
- Soft-boiled eggs, halved
- Green onions (scallions), thinly sliced
- Nori (seaweed sheets), cut into halves or quarters
- Bamboo shoots (menma)
- Optional: spinach, bean sprouts, corn kernels

For Garnish:

- Toasted sesame seeds
- Chili oil or chili flakes (optional)

Instructions:

1. Prepare the Garlic Broth:

- In a large pot, heat sesame oil over medium heat. Add minced garlic and sauté for 1-2 minutes until fragrant and lightly golden.
- Pour in chicken or vegetable broth and water. Add soy sauce, mirin, rice vinegar, and sugar.
- Bring the mixture to a boil, then reduce heat to low and let it simmer for 15-20 minutes to allow the flavors to meld together.
- Season with salt and pepper to taste. Keep the broth hot while preparing the noodles and toppings.

2. Prepare the Ramen Toppings:

- Cook the ramen noodles according to package instructions. Drain and rinse briefly under cold water to remove excess starch.
- If using chashu pork slices or roasted pork belly, slice thinly.
- Soft-boil the eggs: Bring a pot of water to a boil, gently lower eggs into the water, and cook for 7 minutes. Transfer to an ice bath to stop cooking, then peel and halve them.
- Prepare other toppings like thinly sliced green onions (scallions), nori (seaweed sheets), bamboo shoots (menma), and any additional toppings you prefer.

3. Assemble Garlic Ramen:

- Divide the cooked ramen noodles among serving bowls.
- Ladle the hot garlic broth over the noodles.
- Arrange chashu pork slices or roasted pork belly, soft-boiled eggs, green onions (scallions), nori (seaweed sheets), bamboo shoots (menma), and any other toppings you prepared on top of the noodles.
- Optionally, add spinach, bean sprouts, corn kernels, or additional garnishes like toasted sesame seeds and a drizzle of chili oil or chili flakes for extra spice.

4. Serve:

- Serve hot and enjoy your homemade Garlic Ramen!

Notes:

- **Garlic Intensity:** The amount of garlic can be adjusted according to your preference. Start with less if you prefer a milder garlic flavor, or add more for a stronger garlic kick.
- **Broth Variation:** For a richer broth, you can add chicken or pork bones to the broth and simmer for longer to extract more depth of flavor.
- **Noodles:** Fresh ramen noodles are recommended for their texture, but dried noodles can also be used. Follow package instructions for cooking times.
- **Make Ahead:** The garlic broth can be made ahead of time and stored in the refrigerator. Reheat gently before serving.

This Garlic Ramen recipe offers a comforting bowl of noodles with a robust garlic flavor that will warm you up and satisfy your taste buds. Enjoy the savory goodness of homemade ramen!

Sesame Ramen

Ingredients:

For the Sesame Broth:

- 4 cups chicken or vegetable broth (homemade or store-bought)
- 2 cups water
- 3 tablespoons sesame paste (tahini)
- 2 tablespoons soy sauce
- 1 tablespoon sesame oil
- 1 tablespoon mirin (Japanese sweet rice wine)
- 2 cloves garlic, minced
- 1-inch piece ginger, grated
- 1 tablespoon rice vinegar
- 1 teaspoon sugar
- Salt and pepper, to taste

For the Ramen:

- 300g ramen noodles (fresh or dried)
- Chashu pork slices or roasted pork belly (optional)
- Soft-boiled eggs, halved
- Green onions (scallions), thinly sliced
- Nori (seaweed sheets), cut into halves or quarters
- Bamboo shoots (menma)
- Optional: spinach, bean sprouts, corn kernels

For Garnish:

- Toasted sesame seeds
- Sliced fresh chili (optional)

Instructions:

1. Prepare the Sesame Broth:

- In a large pot, combine chicken or vegetable broth and water.
- Add sesame paste (tahini), soy sauce, sesame oil, mirin, minced garlic, grated ginger, rice vinegar, and sugar.
- Bring the mixture to a boil over medium-high heat. Reduce heat to low and let it simmer for about 15-20 minutes to allow the flavors to meld together.
- Season with salt and pepper to taste. Keep the broth hot while preparing the noodles and toppings.

2. Prepare the Ramen Toppings:

- Cook the ramen noodles according to package instructions. Drain and rinse briefly under cold water to remove excess starch.
- If using chashu pork slices or roasted pork belly, slice thinly.
- Soft-boil the eggs: Bring a pot of water to a boil, gently lower eggs into the water, and cook for 7 minutes. Transfer to an ice bath to stop cooking, then peel and halve them.
- Prepare other toppings like thinly sliced green onions (scallions), nori (seaweed sheets), bamboo shoots (menma), and any additional toppings you prefer.

3. Assemble Sesame Ramen:

- Divide the cooked ramen noodles among serving bowls.
- Ladle the hot sesame broth over the noodles.
- Arrange chashu pork slices or roasted pork belly, soft-boiled eggs, green onions (scallions), nori (seaweed sheets), bamboo shoots (menma), and any other toppings you prepared on top of the noodles.
- Optionally, add spinach, bean sprouts, corn kernels, or additional garnishes like toasted sesame seeds and sliced fresh chili for extra flavor and spice.

4. Serve:

- Serve hot and enjoy your homemade Sesame Ramen!

Notes:

- **Sesame Paste (Tahini):** Use smooth sesame paste (tahini) for the broth. It adds a rich nutty flavor to the ramen.
- **Broth Variation:** If you prefer a thicker broth, you can add more sesame paste (tahini) or adjust the consistency with a cornstarch slurry (mix cornstarch with cold water and stir into the broth).
- **Noodles:** Fresh ramen noodles are recommended for their texture, but dried noodles can also be used. Follow package instructions for cooking times.
- **Make Ahead:** The sesame broth can be made ahead of time and stored in the refrigerator. Reheat gently before serving.

Enjoy the nutty and aromatic flavors of Sesame Ramen with its delicious combination of sesame-infused broth and hearty ramen noodles. It's a comforting dish that's perfect for any day!

Duck Ramen

Ingredients:

For the Duck Broth:

- 4 cups chicken or duck broth (homemade or store-bought)
- 2 cups water
- 1 duck leg or breast, skin removed
- 1 onion, quartered
- 2 cloves garlic, smashed
- 1-inch piece ginger, sliced
- 2 tablespoons soy sauce
- 1 tablespoon mirin (Japanese sweet rice wine)
- 1 tablespoon sake (Japanese rice wine)
- 1 tablespoon sesame oil
- Salt and pepper, to taste

For the Ramen:

- 300g ramen noodles (fresh or dried)
- Soft-boiled eggs, halved
- Baby bok choy, halved or quartered
- Green onions (scallions), thinly sliced
- Nori (seaweed sheets), cut into halves or quarters
- Bamboo shoots (menma)
- Optional: corn kernels, bean sprouts, sesame seeds

Instructions:

1. Prepare the Duck Broth:

- In a large pot, combine chicken or duck broth and water.
- Add duck leg or breast, onion, garlic, ginger, soy sauce, mirin, sake, and sesame oil.
- Bring the mixture to a boil over medium-high heat. Skim off any foam that rises to the surface.
- Reduce heat to low, cover, and simmer for 1.5 to 2 hours until the duck meat is tender and falls off the bone.
- Remove the duck meat from the broth. Shred or slice the meat and set aside. Discard the bones and any solids from the broth.
- Season the broth with salt and pepper to taste. Keep the broth hot while preparing the noodles and toppings.

2. Prepare the Ramen Toppings:

- Cook the ramen noodles according to package instructions. Drain and rinse briefly under cold water to remove excess starch.
- Blanch baby bok choy in boiling water for 1-2 minutes until tender-crisp. Drain and set aside.
- Soft-boil the eggs: Bring a pot of water to a boil, gently lower eggs into the water, and cook for 7 minutes. Transfer to an ice bath to stop cooking, then peel and halve them.
- Prepare other toppings like thinly sliced green onions (scallions), nori (seaweed sheets), bamboo shoots (menma), and any additional toppings you prefer.

3. Assemble Duck Ramen:

- Divide the cooked ramen noodles among serving bowls.
- Ladle the hot duck broth over the noodles.
- Arrange shredded or sliced duck meat, soft-boiled eggs, blanched baby bok choy, green onions (scallions), nori (seaweed sheets), bamboo shoots (menma), and any other toppings you prepared on top of the noodles.
- Optionally, add corn kernels, bean sprouts, sesame seeds, or additional garnishes of your choice.

4. Serve:

- Serve hot and enjoy your homemade Duck Ramen!

Notes:

- **Duck Preparation:** Cooking the duck leg or breast in the broth adds rich flavor. You can also roast or grill the duck separately before adding it to the ramen.
- **Broth Variation:** For a deeper flavor, you can roast the duck bones and vegetables before simmering them in the broth.
- **Noodles:** Fresh ramen noodles are recommended for their texture, but dried noodles can also be used. Follow package instructions for cooking times.
- **Make Ahead:** The duck broth can be made ahead of time and stored in the refrigerator. Reheat gently before serving.

Enjoy the rich and savory flavors of Duck Ramen with its tender duck meat and hearty broth. It's a satisfying dish that's sure to impress!

Soba Noodle Ramen

Ingredients:

For the Broth:

- 4 cups chicken or vegetable broth (homemade or store-bought)
- 2 cups water
- 2 tablespoons soy sauce
- 1 tablespoon mirin (Japanese sweet rice wine)
- 1 tablespoon sesame oil
- 2 cloves garlic, minced
- 1-inch piece ginger, grated
- Salt and pepper, to taste

For the Ramen:

- 300g soba noodles
- Chashu pork slices or roasted pork belly (optional)
- Soft-boiled eggs, halved
- Green onions (scallions), thinly sliced
- Nori (seaweed sheets), cut into halves or quarters
- Bamboo shoots (menma)
- Optional: spinach, bean sprouts, corn kernels

For Garnish:

- Toasted sesame seeds
- Shichimi togarashi (Japanese seven spice blend), for extra spice (optional)

Instructions:

1. Prepare the Broth:

- In a large pot, combine chicken or vegetable broth and water.
- Add soy sauce, mirin, sesame oil, minced garlic, and grated ginger.
- Bring the mixture to a boil over medium-high heat. Reduce heat to low and let it simmer for about 15-20 minutes to allow the flavors to meld together.
- Season with salt and pepper to taste. Keep the broth hot while preparing the noodles and toppings.

2. Prepare the Ramen Toppings:

- Cook soba noodles according to package instructions. Drain and rinse under cold water to remove excess starch. Set aside.
- If using chashu pork slices or roasted pork belly, slice thinly.

- Soft-boil the eggs: Bring a pot of water to a boil, gently lower eggs into the water, and cook for 7 minutes. Transfer to an ice bath to stop cooking, then peel and halve them.
- Prepare other toppings like thinly sliced green onions (scallions), nori (seaweed sheets), bamboo shoots (menma), and any additional toppings you prefer.

3. Assemble Soba Noodle Ramen:

- Divide the cooked soba noodles among serving bowls.
- Ladle the hot broth over the noodles.
- Arrange chashu pork slices or roasted pork belly, soft-boiled eggs, green onions (scallions), nori (seaweed sheets), bamboo shoots (menma), and any other toppings you prepared on top of the noodles.
- Optionally, add spinach, bean sprouts, corn kernels, or other vegetables for added texture and flavor.

4. Serve:

- Garnish with toasted sesame seeds and shichimi togarashi (Japanese seven spice blend) for extra spice, if desired.
- Serve hot and enjoy your homemade Soba Noodle Ramen!

Notes:

- **Soba Noodles:** Soba noodles are made from buckwheat flour and have a nutty flavor. They cook quickly and are gluten-free, making them a healthy alternative to traditional ramen noodles.
- **Broth Variation:** For a richer broth, you can add dried shiitake mushrooms or kombu (dried kelp) to the broth while simmering.
- **Make Ahead:** The broth can be made ahead of time and stored in the refrigerator. Reheat gently before serving.

This Soba Noodle Ramen recipe offers a delightful blend of flavors and textures, combining the nuttiness of soba noodles with the savory broth and a variety of toppings. It's a satisfying dish that's perfect for any occasion!

Beef Ramen

Ingredients:

For the Beef Broth:

- 4 cups beef broth (homemade or store-bought)
- 2 cups water
- 2 tablespoons soy sauce
- 1 tablespoon mirin (Japanese sweet rice wine)
- 1 tablespoon sesame oil
- 2 cloves garlic, minced
- 1-inch piece ginger, grated
- 1 onion, sliced
- 1 carrot, sliced
- Salt and pepper, to taste

For the Ramen:

- 300g ramen noodles (fresh or dried)
- Thinly sliced beef (such as ribeye or sirloin)
- Soft-boiled eggs, halved
- Green onions (scallions), thinly sliced
- Nori (seaweed sheets), cut into halves or quarters
- Bamboo shoots (menma)
- Optional: spinach, bean sprouts, corn kernels

For Garnish:

- Toasted sesame seeds
- Shichimi togarashi (Japanese seven spice blend), for extra spice (optional)

Instructions:

1. Prepare the Beef Broth:

- In a large pot, combine beef broth and water.
- Add soy sauce, mirin, sesame oil, minced garlic, grated ginger, sliced onion, and sliced carrot.
- Bring the mixture to a boil over medium-high heat. Reduce heat to low and let it simmer for about 30-45 minutes to allow the flavors to meld together.
- Season with salt and pepper to taste. Keep the broth hot while preparing the noodles and toppings.

2. Prepare the Ramen Toppings:

- Cook the ramen noodles according to package instructions. Drain and rinse briefly under cold water to remove excess starch.
- Thinly slice the beef against the grain. You can either cook the beef slices in the broth or quickly stir-fry them in a separate pan until browned and cooked to your liking.
- Soft-boil the eggs: Bring a pot of water to a boil, gently lower eggs into the water, and cook for 7 minutes. Transfer to an ice bath to stop cooking, then peel and halve them.
- Prepare other toppings like thinly sliced green onions (scallions), nori (seaweed sheets), bamboo shoots (menma), and any additional toppings you prefer.

3. Assemble Beef Ramen:

- Divide the cooked ramen noodles among serving bowls.
- Ladle the hot beef broth over the noodles.
- Arrange thinly sliced beef, soft-boiled eggs, green onions (scallions), nori (seaweed sheets), bamboo shoots (menma), and any other toppings you prepared on top of the noodles.
- Optionally, add spinach, bean sprouts, corn kernels, or other vegetables for added texture and flavor.

4. Serve:

- Garnish with toasted sesame seeds and shichimi togarashi (Japanese seven spice blend) for extra spice, if desired.
- Serve hot and enjoy your homemade Beef Ramen!

Notes:

- **Beef Slices:** For tender beef, ensure to slice it thinly against the grain. You can also marinate the beef slices in soy sauce and sesame oil for added flavor before cooking.
- **Broth Variation:** For a deeper flavor, you can roast beef bones or use beef marrow bones to make the broth.
- **Noodles:** Fresh ramen noodles are recommended for their texture, but dried noodles can also be used. Follow package instructions for cooking times.
- **Make Ahead:** The beef broth can be made ahead of time and stored in the refrigerator. Reheat gently before serving.

Enjoy the robust flavors and comforting warmth of homemade Beef Ramen with its tender beef slices and savory broth. It's a delicious meal that's sure to satisfy!

Natto Ramen

Ingredients:

For the Broth:

- 4 cups chicken or vegetable broth (homemade or store-bought)
- 2 cups water
- 2 tablespoons soy sauce
- 1 tablespoon mirin (Japanese sweet rice wine)
- 1 tablespoon sesame oil
- 2 cloves garlic, minced
- 1-inch piece ginger, grated
- Salt and pepper, to taste

For the Ramen:

- 300g ramen noodles (fresh or dried)
- Natto (fermented soybeans), 1-2 servings per person
- Soft-boiled eggs, halved
- Green onions (scallions), thinly sliced
- Nori (seaweed sheets), cut into halves or quarters
- Bamboo shoots (menma)
- Optional: spinach, bean sprouts, corn kernels

For Garnish:

- Toasted sesame seeds
- Shichimi togarashi (Japanese seven spice blend), for extra spice (optional)

Instructions:

1. Prepare the Broth:

- In a large pot, combine chicken or vegetable broth and water.
- Add soy sauce, mirin, sesame oil, minced garlic, and grated ginger.
- Bring the mixture to a boil over medium-high heat. Reduce heat to low and let it simmer for about 15-20 minutes to allow the flavors to meld together.
- Season with salt and pepper to taste. Keep the broth hot while preparing the noodles and toppings.

2. Prepare the Ramen Toppings:

- Cook the ramen noodles according to package instructions. Drain and rinse briefly under cold water to remove excess starch.

- Prepare natto by mixing it with the accompanying sauce and mustard packet (if included). Stir until well combined.
- Soft-boil the eggs: Bring a pot of water to a boil, gently lower eggs into the water, and cook for 7 minutes. Transfer to an ice bath to stop cooking, then peel and halve them.
- Prepare other toppings like thinly sliced green onions (scallions), nori (seaweed sheets), bamboo shoots (menma), and any additional toppings you prefer.

3. Assemble Natto Ramen:

- Divide the cooked ramen noodles among serving bowls.
- Ladle the hot broth over the noodles.
- Top with servings of prepared natto, soft-boiled eggs, green onions (scallions), nori (seaweed sheets), bamboo shoots (menma), and any other toppings you prepared on top of the noodles.
- Optionally, add spinach, bean sprouts, corn kernels, or other vegetables for added texture and flavor.

4. Serve:

- Garnish with toasted sesame seeds and shichimi togarashi (Japanese seven spice blend) for extra spice, if desired.
- Serve hot and enjoy your homemade Natto Ramen!

Notes:

- **Natto Preparation:** Natto has a distinctive flavor and texture due to its fermentation process. Mix it well with the sauce and mustard provided to incorporate flavors evenly.
- **Broth Variation:** You can enhance the broth with additional umami flavors by adding dried shiitake mushrooms or kombu (dried kelp) while simmering.
- **Noodles:** Fresh ramen noodles are recommended for their texture, but dried noodles can also be used. Follow package instructions for cooking times.
- **Make Ahead:** The broth can be made ahead of time and stored in the refrigerator. Reheat gently before serving.

Enjoy the unique and nutritious flavors of Natto Ramen, featuring the savory umami of natto combined with the comforting elements of ramen. It's a satisfying and wholesome dish that's perfect for exploring Japanese cuisine at home!

Black Garlic Ramen

Ingredients:

For the Broth:

- 4 cups chicken or vegetable broth (homemade or store-bought)
- 2 cups water
- 1 head of black garlic, cloves peeled and minced (around 8-10 cloves)
- 2 tablespoons soy sauce
- 1 tablespoon mirin (Japanese sweet rice wine)
- 1 tablespoon sesame oil
- 1 tablespoon miso paste (white or red)
- 1 tablespoon rice vinegar
- 1 teaspoon sugar
- Salt and pepper, to taste

For the Ramen:

- 300g ramen noodles (fresh or dried)
- Chashu pork slices or roasted pork belly (optional)
- Soft-boiled eggs, halved
- Green onions (scallions), thinly sliced
- Nori (seaweed sheets), cut into halves or quarters
- Bamboo shoots (menma)
- Optional: spinach, bean sprouts, corn kernels

For Garnish:

- Toasted sesame seeds
- Shichimi togarashi (Japanese seven spice blend), for extra spice (optional)

Instructions:

1. Prepare the Broth:

- In a large pot, combine chicken or vegetable broth and water.
- Add minced black garlic cloves, soy sauce, mirin, sesame oil, miso paste, rice vinegar, and sugar.
- Bring the mixture to a boil over medium-high heat. Reduce heat to low and let it simmer for about 15-20 minutes to allow the flavors to meld together.
- Taste and adjust seasoning with salt and pepper as needed. Keep the broth hot while preparing the noodles and toppings.

2. Prepare the Ramen Toppings:

- Cook the ramen noodles according to package instructions. Drain and rinse briefly under cold water to remove excess starch.
- If using chashu pork slices or roasted pork belly, slice thinly.
- Soft-boil the eggs: Bring a pot of water to a boil, gently lower eggs into the water, and cook for 7 minutes. Transfer to an ice bath to stop cooking, then peel and halve them.
- Prepare other toppings like thinly sliced green onions (scallions), nori (seaweed sheets), bamboo shoots (menma), and any additional toppings you prefer.

3. Assemble Black Garlic Ramen:

- Divide the cooked ramen noodles among serving bowls.
- Ladle the hot black garlic broth over the noodles.
- Arrange chashu pork slices or roasted pork belly, soft-boiled eggs, green onions (scallions), nori (seaweed sheets), bamboo shoots (menma), and any other toppings you prepared on top of the noodles.
- Optionally, add spinach, bean sprouts, corn kernels, or other vegetables for added texture and flavor.

4. Serve:

- Garnish with toasted sesame seeds and shichimi togarashi (Japanese seven spice blend) for extra spice, if desired.
- Serve hot and enjoy your homemade Black Garlic Ramen!

Notes:

- **Black Garlic:** Black garlic has a sweet and slightly tangy flavor due to its fermentation process. It adds a unique depth of flavor to the ramen broth.
- **Broth Variation:** For an even richer broth, you can add dried shiitake mushrooms or kombu (dried kelp) while simmering.
- **Noodles:** Fresh ramen noodles are recommended for their texture, but dried noodles can also be used. Follow package instructions for cooking times.
- **Make Ahead:** The black garlic broth can be made ahead of time and stored in the refrigerator. Reheat gently before serving.

Enjoy the rich, sweet, and savory flavors of homemade Black Garlic Ramen with its distinctive black garlic broth and delicious toppings. It's a gourmet twist on traditional ramen that's sure to impress!

Shrimp Ramen

Ingredients:

For the Broth:

- 4 cups chicken or seafood broth (homemade or store-bought)
- 2 cups water
- 2 tablespoons soy sauce
- 1 tablespoon mirin (Japanese sweet rice wine)
- 1 tablespoon sesame oil
- 2 cloves garlic, minced
- 1-inch piece ginger, grated
- Salt and pepper, to taste

For the Ramen:

- 300g ramen noodles (fresh or dried)
- Shrimp, peeled and deveined (about 200-300g)
- Soft-boiled eggs, halved
- Green onions (scallions), thinly sliced
- Nori (seaweed sheets), cut into halves or quarters
- Bamboo shoots (menma)
- Optional: spinach, bean sprouts, corn kernels

For Garnish:

- Toasted sesame seeds
- Shichimi togarashi (Japanese seven spice blend), for extra spice (optional)

Instructions:

1. Prepare the Broth:

- In a large pot, combine chicken or seafood broth and water.
- Add soy sauce, mirin, sesame oil, minced garlic, and grated ginger.
- Bring the mixture to a boil over medium-high heat. Reduce heat to low and let it simmer for about 15-20 minutes to allow the flavors to meld together.
- Season with salt and pepper to taste. Keep the broth hot while preparing the noodles and shrimp.

2. Prepare the Ramen Toppings:

- Cook the ramen noodles according to package instructions. Drain and rinse briefly under cold water to remove excess starch.

- Season shrimp with a little salt and pepper. In a separate pan, heat a bit of oil over medium-high heat and sauté shrimp until pink and cooked through, about 2-3 minutes per side. Set aside.
- Soft-boil the eggs: Bring a pot of water to a boil, gently lower eggs into the water, and cook for 7 minutes. Transfer to an ice bath to stop cooking, then peel and halve them.
- Prepare other toppings like thinly sliced green onions (scallions), nori (seaweed sheets), bamboo shoots (menma), and any additional toppings you prefer.

3. Assemble Shrimp Ramen:

- Divide the cooked ramen noodles among serving bowls.
- Ladle the hot broth over the noodles.
- Arrange cooked shrimp, soft-boiled eggs, green onions (scallions), nori (seaweed sheets), bamboo shoots (menma), and any other toppings you prepared on top of the noodles.
- Optionally, add spinach, bean sprouts, corn kernels, or other vegetables for added texture and flavor.

4. Serve:

- Garnish with toasted sesame seeds and shichimi togarashi (Japanese seven spice blend) for extra spice, if desired.
- Serve hot and enjoy your homemade Shrimp Ramen!

Notes:

- **Shrimp:** Use fresh or thawed shrimp for best results. You can also marinate shrimp with soy sauce and a touch of sesame oil for extra flavor before cooking.
- **Broth Variation:** For a seafood twist, you can use seafood broth instead of chicken broth. Adding a dashi packet or seafood seasoning can enhance the seafood flavor.
- **Noodles:** Fresh ramen noodles are recommended for their texture, but dried noodles can also be used. Follow package instructions for cooking times.
- **Make Ahead:** The broth can be made ahead of time and stored in the refrigerator. Reheat gently before serving.

Enjoy the delicious flavors of Shrimp Ramen with its succulent shrimp, savory broth, and assortment of toppings. It's a satisfying and comforting meal that's perfect for any occasion!

Pork Miso Ramen

Ingredients:

For the Broth:

- 4 cups pork or chicken broth (homemade or store-bought)
- 2 cups water
- 3 tablespoons miso paste (white or red miso)
- 1 tablespoon soy sauce
- 1 tablespoon mirin (Japanese sweet rice wine)
- 1 tablespoon sesame oil
- 2 cloves garlic, minced
- 1-inch piece ginger, grated
- Salt and pepper, to taste

For the Ramen:

- 300g ramen noodles (fresh or dried)
- Chashu pork slices or roasted pork belly (see note below)
- Soft-boiled eggs, halved
- Green onions (scallions), thinly sliced
- Nori (seaweed sheets), cut into halves or quarters
- Bamboo shoots (menma)
- Optional: spinach, bean sprouts, corn kernels

For Garnish:

- Toasted sesame seeds
- Shichimi togarashi (Japanese seven spice blend), for extra spice (optional)

Instructions:

1. Prepare the Broth:

- In a large pot, combine pork or chicken broth and water.
- Add miso paste, soy sauce, mirin, sesame oil, minced garlic, and grated ginger.
- Bring the mixture to a boil over medium-high heat. Reduce heat to low and let it simmer for about 15-20 minutes to allow the flavors to meld together.
- Taste and adjust seasoning with salt and pepper as needed. Keep the broth hot while preparing the noodles and toppings.

2. Prepare the Ramen Toppings:

- Cook the ramen noodles according to package instructions. Drain and rinse briefly under cold water to remove excess starch.

- If using chashu pork slices or roasted pork belly, slice thinly.
- Soft-boil the eggs: Bring a pot of water to a boil, gently lower eggs into the water, and cook for 7 minutes. Transfer to an ice bath to stop cooking, then peel and halve them.
- Prepare other toppings like thinly sliced green onions (scallions), nori (seaweed sheets), bamboo shoots (menma), and any additional toppings you prefer.

3. Assemble Pork Miso Ramen:

- Divide the cooked ramen noodles among serving bowls.
- Ladle the hot miso broth over the noodles.
- Arrange chashu pork slices or roasted pork belly, soft-boiled eggs, green onions (scallions), nori (seaweed sheets), bamboo shoots (menma), and any other toppings you prepared on top of the noodles.
- Optionally, add spinach, bean sprouts, corn kernels, or other vegetables for added texture and flavor.

4. Serve:

- Garnish with toasted sesame seeds and shichimi togarashi (Japanese seven spice blend) for extra spice, if desired.
- Serve hot and enjoy your homemade Pork Miso Ramen!

Notes:

- **Pork:** For chashu pork slices, you can prepare them by marinating pork belly or pork shoulder in a mixture of soy sauce, mirin, sake, sugar, garlic, and ginger, then slow-cooking until tender. Alternatively, you can use roasted pork belly or any leftover pork you have.
- **Miso Paste:** White miso (shiro miso) tends to be milder and sweeter, while red miso (aka miso) is deeper and saltier. Adjust the amount according to your preference.
- **Noodles:** Fresh ramen noodles are recommended for their texture, but dried noodles can also be used. Follow package instructions for cooking times.
- **Make Ahead:** The miso broth can be made ahead of time and stored in the refrigerator. Reheat gently before serving.

Enjoy the rich and comforting flavors of Pork Miso Ramen with its savory miso broth, tender pork slices, and assortment of toppings. It's a satisfying meal that's perfect for a cozy night in!

Vegan Ramen

Ingredients:

For the Broth:

- 4 cups vegetable broth (homemade or store-bought)
- 2 cups water
- 2 tablespoons soy sauce (or tamari for gluten-free)
- 1 tablespoon miso paste (white or red)
- 1 tablespoon sesame oil
- 2 cloves garlic, minced
- 1-inch piece ginger, grated
- 1 onion, sliced
- 1 carrot, sliced
- 1-2 dried shiitake mushrooms (optional, for extra umami)
- Salt and pepper, to taste

For the Ramen:

- 300g ramen noodles (fresh or dried, ensure they are vegan)
- Tofu, sliced and pan-fried or baked until golden
- Soft-boiled eggs (optional, omit for vegan version)
- Green onions (scallions), thinly sliced
- Nori (seaweed sheets), cut into halves or quarters
- Bamboo shoots (menma)
- Optional: spinach, bean sprouts, corn kernels, mushrooms

For Garnish:

- Toasted sesame seeds
- Nori strips
- Chili oil or sriracha (optional, for added spice)

Instructions:

1. Prepare the Broth:

- In a large pot, combine vegetable broth and water.
- Add soy sauce, miso paste, sesame oil, minced garlic, grated ginger, sliced onion, sliced carrot, and dried shiitake mushrooms (if using).
- Bring the mixture to a boil over medium-high heat. Reduce heat to low and let it simmer for about 30 minutes to allow the flavors to meld together. Remove the dried shiitake mushrooms before serving (if used).

- Season with salt and pepper to taste. Keep the broth hot while preparing the noodles and toppings.

2. Prepare the Ramen Toppings:

- Cook the ramen noodles according to package instructions. Drain and rinse briefly under cold water to remove excess starch.
- Slice tofu into thin slices and pan-fry or bake until golden and crispy on both sides.
- Prepare other toppings like thinly sliced green onions (scallions), nori (seaweed sheets), bamboo shoots (menma), and any additional toppings you prefer.

3. Assemble Vegan Ramen:

- Divide the cooked ramen noodles among serving bowls.
- Ladle the hot broth over the noodles.
- Arrange pan-fried tofu slices, green onions (scallions), nori (seaweed sheets), bamboo shoots (menma), and any other toppings you prepared on top of the noodles.
- Optionally, add spinach, bean sprouts, corn kernels, mushrooms, or any other vegetables for added texture and flavor.

4. Serve:

- Garnish with toasted sesame seeds, nori strips, and a drizzle of chili oil or sriracha for added spice, if desired.
- Serve hot and enjoy your homemade Vegan Ramen!

Notes:

- **Tofu:** Use firm or extra firm tofu for best results. Pressing the tofu before cooking helps remove excess moisture and allows it to crisp up better.
- **Broth Variation:** For an even richer broth, you can add kombu (dried kelp) or additional vegetables like celery and leeks while simmering.
- **Noodles:** Ensure the ramen noodles you choose are vegan-friendly, as some may contain egg. Fresh ramen noodles are recommended for their texture, but dried noodles can also be used. Follow package instructions for cooking times.
- **Make Ahead:** The vegetable broth can be made ahead of time and stored in the refrigerator. Reheat gently before serving.

Enjoy the comforting and flavorful Vegan Ramen with its hearty broth, crispy tofu, and assortment of nutritious toppings. It's a perfect dish for vegans and non-vegans alike!

Hakata Ramen

Ingredients:

For the Tonkotsu Broth:

- 6-8 cups water
- 1 lb pork bones (neck bones, trotters, or a mix)
- 2 cloves garlic, crushed
- 1-inch piece ginger, sliced
- 2 green onions (scallions), chopped
- 1 onion, peeled and halved
- 1 carrot, chopped (optional)
- Salt, to taste

For the Ramen:

- 300g fresh Hakata-style ramen noodles (or dried ramen noodles)
- Chashu pork slices (see note below)
- Soft-boiled eggs, halved
- Menma (bamboo shoots)
- Green onions (scallions), thinly sliced
- Nori (seaweed sheets), cut into halves or quarters
- Red pickled ginger (beni shoga), for garnish (optional)

For Chashu Pork:

- 1 lb pork belly or pork shoulder
- 1/2 cup soy sauce
- 1/2 cup mirin (Japanese sweet rice wine)
- 1/4 cup sake
- 1/4 cup sugar
- 2 cups water (or enough to cover the pork)

Instructions:

1. Prepare the Tonkotsu Broth:

- In a large pot, bring water to a boil. Add pork bones and boil vigorously for 10 minutes. This helps to remove impurities and create a cleaner broth.
- Drain the bones and rinse them well under cold water to remove any remaining impurities.
- Return the bones to the pot and add fresh water, garlic, ginger, green onions, onion, and carrot (if using). Bring to a boil, then reduce heat to low and simmer gently for 6-8 hours, skimming off any foam and fat that rises to the surface.

- After simmering, strain the broth through a fine-mesh sieve or cheesecloth. Discard solids. Season with salt to taste. Keep the broth hot while preparing the noodles and toppings.

2. Prepare the Chashu Pork:

- In a separate pot, combine soy sauce, mirin, sake, sugar, and water. Bring to a boil, then add pork belly or pork shoulder.
- Reduce heat to low and simmer gently for 2-3 hours, or until the pork is tender and can be easily pierced with a fork.
- Remove the pork from the pot and let it cool slightly before slicing thinly.

3. Prepare the Ramen Toppings:

- Cook the ramen noodles according to package instructions. Fresh Hakata-style ramen noodles typically cook quickly (1-2 minutes), so be attentive. Drain and rinse briefly under cold water to remove excess starch.
- Soft-boil the eggs: Bring a pot of water to a boil, gently lower eggs into the water, and cook for 7 minutes. Transfer to an ice bath to stop cooking, then peel and halve them.
- Prepare other toppings like menma (bamboo shoots), thinly sliced green onions (scallions), nori (seaweed sheets), and red pickled ginger (beni shoga).

4. Assemble Hakata Ramen:

- Divide the cooked ramen noodles among serving bowls.
- Ladle the hot tonkotsu broth over the noodles.
- Arrange slices of chashu pork, soft-boiled eggs, menma (bamboo shoots), green onions (scallions), nori (seaweed sheets), and a small amount of red pickled ginger (beni shoga) on top of the noodles.
- Optionally, drizzle a bit of sesame oil or chili oil for extra flavor.

5. Serve:

- Serve hot and enjoy your homemade Hakata Ramen!

Notes:

- **Tonkotsu Broth:** Traditional Hakata Ramen features a creamy and rich tonkotsu broth made from simmering pork bones for several hours. It's key to achieving the characteristic flavor of Hakata-style ramen.
- **Chashu Pork:** Chashu pork is typically marinated and braised until tender. You can prepare it ahead of time for convenience.
- **Noodles:** Hakata-style ramen noodles are thin and straight, with a firm texture. Fresh noodles are preferable, but dried ramen noodles can also be used.
- **Make Ahead:** Both the tonkotsu broth and chashu pork can be made ahead of time and stored in the refrigerator. Reheat gently before serving.

Enjoy the rich and comforting flavors of homemade Hakata Ramen, a beloved Japanese noodle soup that's perfect for enjoying at home!

Hokkaido Ramen

Ingredients:

For the Miso Broth:

- 6 cups chicken or vegetable broth (homemade or store-bought)
- 2 cups water
- 1/2 cup miso paste (red or white, adjust to taste)
- 2 tablespoons soy sauce
- 1 tablespoon sesame oil
- 2 cloves garlic, minced
- 1-inch piece ginger, grated
- Salt and pepper, to taste

For the Ramen:

- 300g ramen noodles (fresh or dried)
- Chashu pork slices or seafood (such as scallops, shrimp, or crab)
- Butter, for topping (about 1 tablespoon per bowl)
- Corn kernels (fresh or canned)
- Soft-boiled eggs, halved
- Green onions (scallions), thinly sliced
- Nori (seaweed sheets), cut into halves or quarters

For Garnish:

- Toasted sesame seeds
- Chili oil or shichimi togarashi (Japanese seven spice blend), for extra spice (optional)

Instructions:

1. Prepare the Miso Broth:

- In a large pot, combine chicken or vegetable broth and water.
- Add miso paste, soy sauce, sesame oil, minced garlic, and grated ginger.
- Bring the mixture to a boil over medium-high heat. Reduce heat to low and let it simmer for about 15-20 minutes to allow the flavors to meld together.
- Taste and adjust seasoning with salt and pepper as needed. Keep the broth hot while preparing the noodles and toppings.

2. Prepare the Ramen Toppings:

- Cook the ramen noodles according to package instructions. Drain and rinse briefly under cold water to remove excess starch.

- If using chashu pork slices or seafood, prepare them by cooking or heating them through separately.
- Prepare other toppings like butter (1 tablespoon per bowl), corn kernels, soft-boiled eggs, thinly sliced green onions (scallions), and nori (seaweed sheets).

3. Assemble Hokkaido Ramen:

- Divide the cooked ramen noodles among serving bowls.
- Ladle the hot miso broth over the noodles.
- Add a tablespoon of butter to each bowl and allow it to melt into the broth.
- Arrange cooked chashu pork slices or seafood, corn kernels, soft-boiled eggs, green onions (scallions), and nori (seaweed sheets) on top of the noodles.
- Optionally, drizzle with chili oil or sprinkle with shichimi togarashi (Japanese seven spice blend) for extra spice.

4. Serve:

- Garnish with toasted sesame seeds.
- Serve hot and enjoy your homemade Hokkaido Ramen!

Notes:

- **Miso Paste:** Hokkaido Ramen traditionally uses a miso-based broth, which can be either red (aka miso) or white miso (shiro miso). Adjust the amount of miso paste according to your preference for saltiness and depth of flavor.
- **Butter and Corn:** The combination of butter and sweet corn is a signature feature of Hokkaido Ramen, adding richness and sweetness to the broth.
- **Noodles:** Fresh ramen noodles are recommended for their texture, but dried noodles can also be used. Follow package instructions for cooking times.
- **Make Ahead:** The miso broth can be made ahead of time and stored in the refrigerator. Reheat gently before serving.

Enjoy the comforting and savory flavors of homemade Hokkaido Ramen, featuring its distinctive miso broth and delicious toppings!

Nagasaki Champon

Ingredients:

For the Champon Broth:

- 6 cups chicken or seafood broth (homemade or store-bought)
- 2 cups water
- 2 tablespoons soy sauce
- 1 tablespoon oyster sauce
- 1 tablespoon sake
- 1 tablespoon mirin (Japanese sweet rice wine)
- 1 tablespoon sesame oil
- 2 cloves garlic, minced
- 1-inch piece ginger, grated
- Salt and pepper, to taste

For the Champon Noodles:

- 300g champon noodles or thick, curly noodles (substitute with ramen noodles if champon noodles are unavailable)

For the Champon Toppings:

- Assorted seafood (shrimp, scallops, squid, mussels)
- Sliced pork belly or chicken breast
- Cabbage, shredded
- Napa cabbage, chopped
- Bean sprouts
- Carrots, thinly sliced
- Green onions (scallions), chopped
- Optional: kamaboko (fish cake slices), narutomaki (fish cake with pink swirls)

For Garnish:

- Toasted sesame seeds
- Shichimi togarashi (Japanese seven spice blend), for extra spice (optional)
- Ajitsuke tamago (marinated soft-boiled eggs, optional)

Instructions:

1. Prepare the Champon Broth:

- In a large pot, combine chicken or seafood broth and water.
- Add soy sauce, oyster sauce, sake, mirin, sesame oil, minced garlic, and grated ginger.

- Bring the mixture to a boil over medium-high heat. Reduce heat to low and let it simmer for about 15-20 minutes to allow the flavors to meld together.
- Taste and adjust seasoning with salt and pepper as needed. Keep the broth hot while preparing the noodles and toppings.

2. **Prepare the Champon Toppings:**

- Cook the champon noodles or substitute with ramen noodles according to package instructions. Drain and set aside.
- Slice assorted seafood into bite-sized pieces. Slice pork belly or chicken breast thinly.
- Heat a bit of oil in a large pan or wok over medium-high heat. Stir-fry the sliced pork or chicken until cooked through.
- Add the shredded cabbage, chopped Napa cabbage, bean sprouts, carrots, and green onions to the pan. Stir-fry for a few minutes until vegetables are slightly wilted.

3. **Assemble Nagasaki Champon:**

- Divide the cooked champon noodles among serving bowls.
- Ladle the hot champon broth over the noodles.
- Arrange the cooked seafood, pork or chicken, stir-fried vegetables, kamaboko, and narutomaki on top of the noodles.
- Optionally, add ajitsuke tamago (marinated soft-boiled eggs) on the side.

4. **Serve:**

- Garnish with toasted sesame seeds and shichimi togarashi (Japanese seven spice blend), if desired.
- Serve hot and enjoy your homemade Nagasaki Champon!

Notes:

- **Champon Noodles:** Champon noodles are a type of thick, curly noodle similar to udon but slightly different in texture. If you can't find champon noodles, you can substitute with thick ramen noodles or udon noodles.
- **Seafood and Meat:** Feel free to customize the protein in your Nagasaki Champon. You can use a combination of seafood like shrimp, scallops, squid, and mussels, along with pork, chicken, or even beef.
- **Make Ahead:** The champon broth can be made ahead of time and stored in the refrigerator. Reheat gently before serving.

Enjoy the comforting and flavorful Nagasaki Champon, a delicious noodle dish that brings together a variety of ingredients in a satisfying seafood broth!

Okinawa Soba

Ingredients:

For the Broth:

- 8 cups dashi stock (homemade or store-bought)
- 2 cups water
- 1/4 cup soy sauce
- 2 tablespoons mirin (Japanese sweet rice wine)
- 1 tablespoon sake
- 2 cloves garlic, minced
- 1-inch piece ginger, sliced
- 1 onion, halved
- Salt, to taste

For the Noodles:

- 300g Okinawa soba noodles (substitute with udon noodles if Okinawa soba noodles are unavailable)

For the Toppings:

- Soki (Okinawan braised pork spare ribs) or thinly sliced pork belly
- Kamaboko (fish cake slices)
- Narutomaki (fish cake with pink swirls)
- Green onions (scallions), chopped
- Beni shoga (red pickled ginger)
- Katsuobushi (dried bonito flakes), for garnish
- Optional: moyashi (bean sprouts), sliced shiitake mushrooms, boiled egg

Instructions:

1. Prepare the Broth:

- In a large pot, combine dashi stock and water.
- Add soy sauce, mirin, sake, minced garlic, sliced ginger, and halved onion.
- Bring the mixture to a boil over medium-high heat. Reduce heat to low and let it simmer for about 30 minutes to allow the flavors to meld together.
- Taste and adjust seasoning with salt if necessary. Keep the broth hot while preparing the noodles and toppings.

2. Prepare the Toppings:

- If using soki (Okinawan braised pork spare ribs), prepare them by braising pork spare ribs in a mixture of soy sauce, sake, mirin, sugar, garlic, and ginger until tender.

- Slice kamaboko (fish cake slices) and narutomaki (fish cake with pink swirls) into thin slices.
- Chop green onions (scallions) and prepare beni shoga (red pickled ginger).

3. Cook the Noodles:

- Cook Okinawa soba noodles (or substitute with udon noodles) according to package instructions. Drain and rinse briefly under cold water to remove excess starch.

4. Assemble Okinawa Soba:

- Divide the cooked noodles among serving bowls.
- Ladle the hot broth over the noodles.
- Arrange soki (braised pork spare ribs), kamaboko, narutomaki, green onions (scallions), beni shoga, and any additional toppings like moyashi (bean sprouts), sliced shiitake mushrooms, or boiled egg on top of the noodles.

5. Serve:

- Garnish each bowl with a sprinkle of katsuobushi (dried bonito flakes) for added umami flavor.
- Serve hot and enjoy your homemade Okinawa Soba!

Notes:

- **Dashi Stock:** Dashi is a Japanese stock made from kombu (dried kelp) and katsuobushi (dried bonito flakes). You can make dashi from scratch or use instant dashi powder for convenience.
- **Noodles:** Okinawa soba noodles are traditionally made from wheat flour and are thicker and chewier compared to udon noodles. If you can't find Okinawa soba noodles, substitute with fresh or dried udon noodles.
- **Toppings:** Feel free to customize the toppings based on your preference and availability. Okinawa Soba often includes various seafood and pork toppings.
- **Make Ahead:** The broth and braised pork spare ribs can be made ahead of time and stored in the refrigerator. Reheat gently before serving.

Enjoy the rich and comforting flavors of homemade Okinawa Soba, a traditional dish that reflects the unique culinary heritage of Okinawa prefecture in Japan!

Tantanmen (Dan Dan Noodles)

Ingredients:

For the Tantanmen Sauce:

- 2 tablespoons sesame paste (or tahini)
- 2 tablespoons soy sauce
- 1 tablespoon miso paste
- 1 tablespoon chili oil (adjust to taste)
- 1 tablespoon rice vinegar
- 1 tablespoon sugar
- 1 clove garlic, minced
- 1-inch piece ginger, grated
- 1 cup chicken or vegetable broth

For the Noodles:

- 300g fresh ramen noodles (or substitute with dried ramen noodles)
- 1 tablespoon sesame oil

For the Toppings:

- 200g ground pork (or substitute with ground chicken or tofu for vegetarian option)
- 2-3 green onions (scallions), thinly sliced
- 1/2 cup bean sprouts
- 2-3 tablespoons chopped cilantro (optional)
- Chili oil or chili paste, for extra spice (optional)
- Toasted sesame seeds, for garnish

Instructions:

1. Prepare the Tantanmen Sauce:

- In a small bowl, whisk together sesame paste (or tahini), soy sauce, miso paste, chili oil, rice vinegar, sugar, minced garlic, grated ginger, and chicken or vegetable broth until smooth. Adjust chili oil according to your desired spice level.

2. Cook the Noodles:

- Cook the fresh ramen noodles in boiling water according to package instructions (usually 1-2 minutes). If using dried ramen noodles, cook according to package instructions until al dente. Drain and rinse under cold water to remove excess starch. Toss with sesame oil to prevent sticking.

3. Prepare the Toppings:

- In a skillet or frying pan, cook ground pork over medium-high heat until browned and cooked through. Break up the pork into smaller pieces as it cooks. Drain excess fat if necessary.
- Add half of the sliced green onions (scallions) to the skillet with the cooked pork and sauté briefly until fragrant.

4. Assemble Tantanmen:

- Divide the cooked noodles among serving bowls.
- Pour the prepared Tantanmen sauce over the noodles.
- Top with the cooked ground pork mixture, remaining sliced green onions (scallions), bean sprouts, and chopped cilantro (if using).
- Optionally, drizzle with additional chili oil or chili paste for extra spice.

5. Serve:

- Garnish with toasted sesame seeds.
- Serve hot and enjoy your homemade Tantanmen (Dan Dan Noodles)!

Notes:

- **Sesame Paste:** Traditional Tantanmen uses Chinese sesame paste, but you can substitute with tahini for a similar nutty flavor.
- **Miso Paste:** Adds depth of flavor to the sauce. Adjust the amount based on your preference.
- **Spice Level:** Adjust the amount of chili oil or chili paste according to your taste. Tantanmen is typically spicy, so feel free to add more for extra heat.
- **Vegetarian Option:** Substitute ground pork with ground chicken or tofu crumbles for a vegetarian version.
- **Make Ahead:** You can prepare the sauce and toppings ahead of time and store them separately in the refrigerator. Reheat the sauce gently before serving over freshly cooked noodles.

Enjoy the rich and savory flavors of homemade Tantanmen, a comforting and satisfying noodle dish with a spicy kick!

Green Curry Ramen

Ingredients:

For the Green Curry Broth:

- 2 tablespoons green curry paste
- 1 can (14 oz) coconut milk
- 4 cups chicken or vegetable broth
- 1 tablespoon fish sauce (optional, for added umami)
- 1 tablespoon soy sauce
- 1 tablespoon brown sugar (or palm sugar)
- Juice of 1 lime
- Salt, to taste

For the Ramen:

- 300g ramen noodles (fresh or dried)
- 1 tablespoon vegetable oil
- 1 onion, thinly sliced
- 1 red bell pepper, thinly sliced
- 1 cup snap peas, trimmed
- 200g firm tofu, cut into cubes
- Fresh basil leaves, for garnish
- Fresh cilantro leaves, for garnish
- Lime wedges, for serving

Instructions:

1. Prepare the Green Curry Broth:

- In a large pot, heat vegetable oil over medium heat. Add green curry paste and sauté for 1-2 minutes until fragrant.
- Stir in coconut milk, chicken or vegetable broth, fish sauce (if using), soy sauce, and brown sugar. Bring to a simmer and let it cook for 10-15 minutes to allow flavors to meld together.
- Stir in lime juice and season with salt to taste. Keep the broth warm while preparing the noodles and toppings.

2. Prepare the Ramen and Toppings:

- Cook ramen noodles according to package instructions. Drain and set aside.
- In a separate pan, heat vegetable oil over medium-high heat. Add onion, red bell pepper, and snap peas. Sauté for 3-4 minutes until vegetables are tender-crisp.

- Add tofu cubes and continue to cook for another 2-3 minutes until tofu is lightly browned and heated through.

3. Assemble Green Curry Ramen:

- Divide cooked ramen noodles among serving bowls.
- Ladle the hot green curry broth over the noodles.
- Top with sautéed vegetables and tofu mixture.

4. Serve:

- Garnish with fresh basil leaves and cilantro leaves.
- Serve hot with lime wedges on the side for squeezing over the ramen.

Notes:

- **Green Curry Paste:** You can find green curry paste in most grocery stores or Asian markets. Adjust the amount according to your desired level of spiciness.
- **Coconut Milk:** Use full-fat coconut milk for a richer and creamier broth.
- **Vegetables and Protein:** Feel free to customize the vegetables and protein based on your preference. You can add mushrooms, baby corn, or chicken instead of tofu.
- **Garnishes:** Fresh herbs like basil and cilantro add brightness to the dish. Lime wedges provide a burst of acidity that complements the rich broth.
- **Make Ahead:** The broth can be prepared ahead of time and stored in the refrigerator for up to 3 days. Reheat gently before serving over freshly cooked noodles and toppings.

Enjoy the fusion of flavors in this Green Curry Ramen, combining the best of Japanese and Thai cuisines in one comforting bowl!

Lobster Ramen

Ingredients:

For the Lobster Broth:

- 2 lobster tails (or 1 whole lobster)
- 6 cups water
- 2 cups chicken or vegetable broth
- 2 cloves garlic, smashed
- 1-inch piece ginger, sliced
- 2 green onions (scallions), chopped
- 1 onion, peeled and halved
- 1 carrot, chopped
- 1 celery stalk, chopped
- 1 tablespoon soy sauce
- Salt and pepper, to taste

For the Ramen:

- 300g ramen noodles (fresh or dried)
- 1 tablespoon vegetable oil
- 1 onion, thinly sliced
- 2 garlic cloves, minced
- 1-inch piece ginger, grated
- 1/2 cup corn kernels (fresh or frozen)
- 1/2 cup shiitake mushrooms, sliced
- 2 cups baby spinach
- 2 soft-boiled eggs, halved
- Nori (seaweed sheets), for garnish
- Toasted sesame seeds, for garnish

Instructions:

1. Prepare the Lobster Broth:

- If using lobster tails, remove the meat from the shells and set aside for later. Reserve the shells.
- In a large pot, combine water, chicken or vegetable broth, lobster shells (and bodies if using whole lobster), smashed garlic, sliced ginger, chopped green onions (scallions), onion, carrot, and celery. Bring to a boil over medium-high heat.
- Reduce heat to low and simmer for 30-45 minutes to extract flavors from the lobster shells and vegetables.
- Strain the broth through a fine-mesh sieve or cheesecloth, discarding solids. Return the strained broth to the pot.

- Stir in soy sauce and season with salt and pepper to taste. Keep the lobster broth warm while preparing the noodles and toppings.

2. Prepare the Ramen and Toppings:

- Cook ramen noodles according to package instructions. Drain and set aside.
- In a separate pan, heat vegetable oil over medium heat. Add onion and sauté until softened, about 3-4 minutes.
- Add minced garlic and grated ginger, cook for another 1-2 minutes until fragrant.
- Stir in corn kernels and shiitake mushrooms, cook for 3-4 minutes until mushrooms are tender.
- Add baby spinach and cook briefly until wilted.

3. Assemble Lobster Ramen:

- Divide cooked ramen noodles among serving bowls.
- Ladle the hot lobster broth over the noodles.
- Top with sautéed vegetables mixture.
- Garnish each bowl with lobster meat (reserved from earlier), soft-boiled egg halves, nori (seaweed sheets), and toasted sesame seeds.

4. Serve:

- Serve hot and enjoy your luxurious Lobster Ramen!

Notes:

- **Lobster:** Fresh lobster adds a delicate and sweet flavor to the broth. You can use lobster tails or a whole lobster depending on availability and preference.
- **Vegetables:** Feel free to customize the vegetables based on your preference. Bok choy, bamboo shoots, or bell peppers can also complement the flavors well.
- **Garnishes:** Nori and toasted sesame seeds add texture and umami to the dish. You can also drizzle with a bit of sesame oil for extra richness.
- **Make Ahead:** The lobster broth can be prepared ahead of time and stored in the refrigerator for up to 2 days. Reheat gently before serving over freshly cooked noodles and toppings.

Enjoy the luxurious and flavorful experience of homemade Lobster Ramen, perfect for a special occasion or a comforting meal at home!

Clam Ramen

Ingredients:

For the Clam Broth:

- 2 dozen littleneck clams, scrubbed clean
- 6 cups water
- 2 cups chicken or vegetable broth
- 2 cloves garlic, minced
- 1-inch piece ginger, sliced
- 2 green onions (scallions), chopped
- 1 tablespoon soy sauce
- 1 tablespoon sake (Japanese rice wine)
- Salt and pepper, to taste

For the Ramen:

- 300g ramen noodles (fresh or dried)
- 1 tablespoon vegetable oil
- 1 onion, thinly sliced
- 2 cloves garlic, minced
- 1-inch piece ginger, grated
- 1/2 cup corn kernels (fresh or frozen)
- 1/2 cup shiitake mushrooms, sliced
- 2 cups baby spinach
- 2 soft-boiled eggs, halved
- Nori (seaweed sheets), for garnish
- Toasted sesame seeds, for garnish

Instructions:

1. Prepare the Clam Broth:

- In a large pot, combine water, chicken or vegetable broth, garlic, ginger, chopped green onions (scallions), soy sauce, and sake. Bring to a boil over medium-high heat.
- Add cleaned littleneck clams to the pot. Cover and cook for 5-7 minutes until clams open. Discard any clams that do not open.
- Remove clams with a slotted spoon and set aside. Strain the broth through a fine-mesh sieve or cheesecloth to remove solids. Return the strained broth to the pot.
- Season the clam broth with salt and pepper to taste. Keep warm while preparing the noodles and toppings.

2. Prepare the Ramen and Toppings:

- Cook ramen noodles according to package instructions. Drain and set aside.
- In a separate pan, heat vegetable oil over medium heat. Add onion and sauté until softened, about 3-4 minutes.
- Add minced garlic and grated ginger, cook for another 1-2 minutes until fragrant.
- Stir in corn kernels and shiitake mushrooms, cook for 3-4 minutes until mushrooms are tender.
- Add baby spinach and cook briefly until wilted.

3. Assemble Clam Ramen:

- Divide cooked ramen noodles among serving bowls.
- Ladle the hot clam broth over the noodles.
- Top with sautéed vegetables mixture.
- Garnish each bowl with cooked littleneck clams, soft-boiled egg halves, nori (seaweed sheets), and toasted sesame seeds.

4. Serve:

- Serve hot and enjoy your flavorful Clam Ramen!

Notes:

- **Clams:** Use fresh littleneck clams for the best flavor. Scrub them thoroughly to remove any sand or grit before cooking.
- **Vegetables:** Feel free to customize the vegetables based on your preference. Bok choy, bamboo shoots, or bean sprouts can also complement the flavors well.
- **Garnishes:** Nori and toasted sesame seeds add texture and umami to the dish. You can also drizzle with a bit of sesame oil for extra richness.
- **Make Ahead:** The clam broth can be prepared ahead of time and stored in the refrigerator for up to 2 days. Reheat gently before serving over freshly cooked noodles and toppings.

Enjoy the briny goodness and comforting warmth of homemade Clam Ramen, perfect for a satisfying meal any time of year!

Chicken Paitan Ramen

Ingredients:

For the Chicken Paitan Broth:

- 2 lbs chicken bones (such as backs, wings, or carcasses)
- 2 tablespoons vegetable oil
- 1 onion, peeled and halved
- 4 cloves garlic, smashed
- 1-inch piece ginger, sliced
- 2 green onions (scallions), chopped
- 8 cups water
- 2 cups chicken broth
- 1 cup whole milk or heavy cream
- Salt, to taste

For the Ramen:

- 300g ramen noodles (fresh or dried)
- 1 tablespoon vegetable oil
- 1 onion, thinly sliced
- 2 cloves garlic, minced
- 1-inch piece ginger, grated
- 1/2 cup bamboo shoots, sliced
- 1/2 cup corn kernels (fresh or frozen)
- 2 cups baby spinach
- 2 soft-boiled eggs, halved
- Nori (seaweed sheets), for garnish
- Toasted sesame seeds, for garnish
- Thinly sliced cooked chicken breast or thigh meat, optional

Instructions:

1. Prepare the Chicken Paitan Broth:

- In a large pot, heat vegetable oil over medium-high heat. Add chicken bones and sear until golden brown, about 5-7 minutes.
- Add onion, garlic, ginger, and chopped green onions (scallions) to the pot. Sauté for another 3-4 minutes until aromatic.
- Pour in water and chicken broth. Bring to a boil, then reduce heat to low and simmer, uncovered, for 3-4 hours. Skim any foam or impurities that rise to the surface.
- Strain the broth through a fine-mesh sieve or cheesecloth into a clean pot, discarding solids. Return the strained broth to the stove.

- Stir in whole milk or heavy cream and simmer gently for another 20-30 minutes to meld flavors together. Season with salt to taste. Keep warm while preparing the noodles and toppings.

2. Prepare the Ramen and Toppings:

- Cook ramen noodles according to package instructions. Drain and set aside.
- In a separate pan, heat vegetable oil over medium heat. Add onion and sauté until softened, about 3-4 minutes.
- Add minced garlic and grated ginger, cook for another 1-2 minutes until fragrant.
- Stir in bamboo shoots and corn kernels, cook for 2-3 minutes until heated through.
- Add baby spinach and cook briefly until wilted.

3. Assemble Chicken Paitan Ramen:

- Divide cooked ramen noodles among serving bowls.
- Ladle the hot Chicken Paitan broth over the noodles.
- Top with sautéed vegetables mixture.
- Arrange soft-boiled egg halves on top. Optionally, add thinly sliced cooked chicken breast or thigh meat.
- Garnish each bowl with nori (seaweed sheets) and toasted sesame seeds.

4. Serve:

- Serve hot and enjoy your creamy and flavorful Chicken Paitan Ramen!

Notes:

- **Chicken Bones:** Using a mix of chicken bones adds depth of flavor to the broth. You can find chicken backs, wings, or carcasses at most butcher shops or supermarkets.
- **Vegetables:** Feel free to customize the vegetables based on your preference. Mushrooms, bean sprouts, or bok choy can also complement the flavors well.
- **Garnishes:** Nori and toasted sesame seeds add texture and umami to the dish. You can also drizzle with a bit of sesame oil for extra richness.
- **Make Ahead:** The Chicken Paitan broth can be prepared ahead of time and stored in the refrigerator for up to 3 days. Reheat gently before serving over freshly cooked noodles and toppings.

Enjoy the comforting and creamy indulgence of homemade Chicken Paitan Ramen, perfect for a satisfying meal any time of year!

Spicy Szechuan Ramen

Ingredients:

For the Broth:

- 6 cups chicken or vegetable broth
- 2 cups water
- 2 tablespoons Szechuan peppercorns
- 4 cloves garlic, minced
- 1-inch piece ginger, sliced
- 2 tablespoons chili bean paste (Doubanjiang)
- 2 tablespoons soy sauce
- 1 tablespoon sesame oil
- 1 tablespoon rice vinegar
- 1 tablespoon sugar
- Salt, to taste

For the Ramen:

- 300g ramen noodles (fresh or dried)
- 1 tablespoon vegetable oil
- 1 onion, thinly sliced
- 1 bell pepper, thinly sliced
- 1 cup shiitake mushrooms, sliced
- 200g firm tofu, cut into cubes
- 2 cups baby spinach
- 2 soft-boiled eggs, halved
- Green onions (scallions), sliced, for garnish
- Toasted sesame seeds, for garnish

Instructions:

1. Prepare the Broth:

- In a large pot, toast Szechuan peppercorns over medium heat until fragrant, about 1-2 minutes. Crush them lightly using a mortar and pestle or the back of a spoon.
- Add chicken or vegetable broth, water, minced garlic, sliced ginger, chili bean paste (Doubanjiang), soy sauce, sesame oil, rice vinegar, and sugar to the pot with the toasted Szechuan peppercorns. Bring to a boil over medium-high heat.
- Reduce heat to low and let the broth simmer for 15-20 minutes to allow the flavors to meld together. Taste and adjust seasoning with salt if needed.

2. Prepare the Ramen and Toppings:

- Cook ramen noodles according to package instructions. Drain and set aside.
- In a separate pan, heat vegetable oil over medium heat. Add onion and bell pepper slices, sauté until softened, about 3-4 minutes.
- Add sliced shiitake mushrooms and tofu cubes, cook for another 3-4 minutes until mushrooms are tender and tofu is heated through.
- Add baby spinach and cook briefly until wilted.

3. Assemble Spicy Szechuan Ramen:

- Divide cooked ramen noodles among serving bowls.
- Ladle the hot Spicy Szechuan broth over the noodles.
- Top with sautéed vegetables and tofu mixture.
- Arrange soft-boiled egg halves on top.

4. Serve:

- Garnish each bowl with sliced green onions (scallions) and toasted sesame seeds.
- Serve hot and enjoy your Spicy Szechuan Ramen!

Notes:

- **Szechuan Peppercorns:** These provide a unique numbing and spicy flavor to the broth. Adjust the amount according to your preference for spiciness.
- **Chili Bean Paste (Doubanjiang):** Adds depth and heat to the broth. Adjust the amount based on your desired level of spiciness.
- **Vegetables and Protein:** Feel free to customize the vegetables and protein based on your preference. Bok choy, bean sprouts, or thinly sliced pork can also complement the flavors well.
- **Garnishes:** Green onions (scallions) and toasted sesame seeds add texture and additional flavor to the ramen.
- **Make Ahead:** The broth can be prepared ahead of time and stored in the refrigerator for up to 3 days. Reheat gently before serving over freshly cooked noodles and toppings.

Enjoy the bold and spicy flavors of homemade Spicy Szechuan Ramen, perfect for a satisfying and warming meal!

Truffle Ramen

Ingredients:

For the Broth:

- 6 cups chicken or vegetable broth
- 2 cups water
- 2 cloves garlic, minced
- 1-inch piece ginger, sliced
- 2 tablespoons soy sauce
- 1 tablespoon mirin (Japanese sweet rice wine)
- 1 tablespoon sesame oil
- Salt and white pepper, to taste
- Truffle oil, to taste (optional, for extra truffle flavor)

For the Ramen:

- 300g ramen noodles (fresh or dried)
- 1 tablespoon vegetable oil
- 1 onion, thinly sliced
- 1 cup shiitake mushrooms, sliced
- 2 cups baby spinach
- 200g firm tofu, cut into cubes (optional, for protein)
- 2 soft-boiled eggs, halved
- Green onions (scallions), thinly sliced, for garnish
- Nori (seaweed sheets), for garnish
- Toasted sesame seeds, for garnish

For Truffle Garnish (optional):

- Truffle slices or truffle paste
- Truffle salt or truffle zest

Instructions:

1. Prepare the Broth:

- In a large pot, combine chicken or vegetable broth, water, minced garlic, sliced ginger, soy sauce, mirin, and sesame oil. Bring to a boil over medium-high heat.
- Reduce heat to low and let the broth simmer for 15-20 minutes to allow flavors to meld together. Season with salt and white pepper to taste.
- Optionally, add a few drops of truffle oil to the broth for extra truffle flavor. Adjust the amount according to your preference.

2. Prepare the Ramen and Toppings:

- Cook ramen noodles according to package instructions. Drain and set aside.
- In a separate pan, heat vegetable oil over medium heat. Add onion and sauté until softened, about 3-4 minutes.
- Add sliced shiitake mushrooms and tofu cubes (if using), cook for another 3-4 minutes until mushrooms are tender.
- Add baby spinach and cook briefly until wilted.

3. Assemble Truffle Ramen:

- Divide cooked ramen noodles among serving bowls.
- Ladle the hot Truffle broth over the noodles.
- Top with sautéed vegetables and tofu mixture.
- Arrange soft-boiled egg halves on top.

4. Garnish and Serve:

- Garnish each bowl with thinly sliced green onions (scallions), nori (seaweed sheets), and toasted sesame seeds.
- If using truffle slices or truffle paste, shave or spread over the ramen bowls. Sprinkle with truffle salt or truffle zest for added aroma.
- Serve hot and enjoy your luxurious Truffle Ramen!

Notes:

- **Truffle Oil:** Use a high-quality truffle oil for the best flavor. Add it sparingly as it can be quite potent.
- **Truffle Garnish:** Fresh truffle slices or truffle paste can elevate the dish with their distinct aroma and flavor. Use them as a finishing touch to enhance the truffle experience.
- **Vegetables and Protein:** Customize the ramen with your favorite vegetables and protein. Mushrooms, bok choy, or thinly sliced pork are also great additions.
- **Make Ahead:** The broth can be prepared ahead of time and stored in the refrigerator for up to 3 days. Reheat gently before serving over freshly cooked noodles and toppings.

Enjoy the decadent and aromatic flavors of homemade Truffle Ramen, perfect for a special occasion or a comforting meal at home!

Tsukemen (Cold Dipping Ramen)

Ingredients:

For the Dipping Broth:

- 4 cups chicken or vegetable broth
- 2 tablespoons soy sauce
- 2 tablespoons mirin (Japanese sweet rice wine)
- 1 tablespoon sake (Japanese rice wine) or dry sherry
- 1 tablespoon sugar
- 1-inch piece ginger, sliced
- 2 cloves garlic, minced
- 1 green onion (scallion), chopped
- 1 teaspoon sesame oil
- Optional: 1/2 teaspoon chili oil or rayu (Japanese chili oil)

For the Ramen:

- 300g ramen noodles (fresh or dried)
- 1 tablespoon vegetable oil
- 1/2 cup bamboo shoots, sliced
- 1/2 cup sliced cooked pork or chicken (optional)
- 2 soft-boiled eggs, halved
- 1 sheet nori (seaweed), cut into small pieces
- Thinly sliced green onions (scallions), for garnish
- Toasted sesame seeds, for garnish

Instructions:

1. Prepare the Dipping Broth:

- In a medium saucepan, combine chicken or vegetable broth, soy sauce, mirin, sake or sherry, sugar, ginger, garlic, and green onion (scallion). Bring to a boil over medium-high heat.
- Reduce heat to low and simmer for 10-15 minutes to allow the flavors to meld together.
- Stir in sesame oil and chili oil (if using). Taste and adjust seasoning if needed. Keep the dipping broth warm while preparing the noodles and toppings.

2. Prepare the Ramen and Toppings:

- Cook ramen noodles according to package instructions. Drain and rinse under cold water to stop the cooking process. Drain well again.
- Arrange noodles on serving plates or bowls. Optionally, you can chill the noodles in ice water briefly before draining to serve them cold.

- Heat vegetable oil in a skillet over medium heat. Add bamboo shoots and sliced pork or chicken (if using). Sauté until heated through.

3. Assemble Tsukemen:

- Divide the hot dipping broth into individual bowls or small serving pots.
- Serve the cooked ramen noodles on a separate plate or bowl.
- Arrange bamboo shoots, sliced pork or chicken (if using), soft-boiled egg halves, nori pieces, and sliced green onions on the side.

4. Serve:

- To eat, take a portion of noodles with chopsticks and dip them into the hot dipping broth. Enjoy the noodles and toppings with the flavorful broth.
- Garnish with toasted sesame seeds for added texture and flavor.

Notes:

- **Dipping Broth Variations:** Feel free to adjust the dipping broth according to your taste preferences. You can add more soy sauce for saltiness, mirin for sweetness, or chili oil for heat.
- **Noodle Texture:** Tsukemen noodles are traditionally served cold or at room temperature. Chilling them briefly in ice water helps them retain a firm texture when dipped in the hot broth.
- **Toppings:** Customize the toppings based on your preferences. Besides bamboo shoots, pork or chicken, you can add blanched spinach, menma (fermented bamboo shoots), or even extra nori.
- **Make Ahead:** Prepare the dipping broth and toppings ahead of time, then assemble the dish just before serving for the best flavor and texture.

Enjoy the unique and satisfying experience of Tsukemen, a refreshing twist on traditional ramen!

Cheese Ramen

Ingredients:

For the Ramen:

- 300g ramen noodles (fresh or dried)
- 4 cups chicken or vegetable broth
- 2 cups water
- 2 cloves garlic, minced
- 1-inch piece ginger, sliced
- 2 tablespoons soy sauce
- 1 tablespoon sesame oil
- Salt and pepper, to taste

For the Cheese Mixture:

- 1 cup shredded cheese (cheddar, mozzarella, or a blend)
- 1/2 cup milk or cream
- 2 tablespoons butter
- Optional: 1 teaspoon chili flakes or sriracha (for heat)

Optional Toppings:

- Soft-boiled eggs, halved
- Sliced green onions (scallions)
- Seaweed (nori), shredded
- Cooked chicken or pork slices

Instructions:

1. Prepare the Ramen:

- Cook ramen noodles according to package instructions. Drain and set aside.
- In a large pot, combine chicken or vegetable broth, water, minced garlic, sliced ginger, soy sauce, and sesame oil. Bring to a boil over medium-high heat.
- Reduce heat to low and simmer for 10-15 minutes to allow the flavors to meld together. Season with salt and pepper to taste.

2. Prepare the Cheese Mixture:

- In a small saucepan, melt butter over medium heat. Add shredded cheese and milk or cream.
- Stir continuously until the cheese is melted and the mixture is smooth and creamy. Add chili flakes or sriracha for a spicy kick if desired. Keep warm over low heat.

3. Assemble Cheese Ramen:

- Divide cooked ramen noodles among serving bowls.
- Ladle the hot broth over the noodles.
- Pour a generous amount of the cheese mixture over the noodles and broth.

4. Serve:

- Garnish each bowl with soft-boiled egg halves, sliced green onions (scallions), shredded seaweed (nori), and cooked chicken or pork slices if desired.
- Serve immediately and enjoy your creamy and comforting Cheese Ramen!

Notes:

- **Cheese:** You can use any type of cheese you prefer or have on hand. Cheddar and mozzarella are popular choices, but feel free to experiment with different cheeses or blends.
- **Spice Level:** Adjust the spiciness of the ramen by adding more or less chili flakes or sriracha to the cheese mixture.
- **Toppings:** Customize your Cheese Ramen with additional toppings like bamboo shoots, corn kernels, or spinach for added texture and flavor.
- **Make Ahead:** Prepare the cheese mixture and broth ahead of time, then assemble the ramen just before serving for the best taste and texture.

Enjoy the indulgent and creamy flavors of homemade Cheese Ramen, perfect for a cozy meal any time of year!

Tom Yum Ramen

Ingredients:

For the Broth:

- 4 cups chicken or vegetable broth
- 2 cups water
- 2 stalks lemongrass, smashed and cut into pieces
- 4-6 kaffir lime leaves
- 3-4 slices galangal or ginger
- 2 cloves garlic, minced
- 2-3 Thai bird's eye chilies, chopped (adjust to taste)
- 2 tablespoons Thai chili paste (Nam Prik Pao)
- 3 tablespoons fish sauce
- 2 tablespoons soy sauce
- 1 tablespoon lime juice
- 1 tablespoon sugar
- Salt, to taste

For the Ramen:

- 300g ramen noodles (fresh or dried)
- 1 tablespoon vegetable oil
- 1 onion, thinly sliced
- 1 bell pepper, thinly sliced
- 1 cup mushrooms (shiitake or button), sliced
- 200g firm tofu, cut into cubes
- 2 cups baby spinach
- 2 soft-boiled eggs, halved
- Fresh cilantro, chopped, for garnish
- Lime wedges, for garnish

Instructions:

1. Prepare the Broth:

- In a large pot, combine chicken or vegetable broth and water. Bring to a boil over medium-high heat.
- Add lemongrass, kaffir lime leaves, galangal or ginger, minced garlic, Thai bird's eye chilies, and Thai chili paste (Nam Prik Pao). Simmer for 10-15 minutes to infuse the flavors.
- Stir in fish sauce, soy sauce, lime juice, and sugar. Taste and adjust seasoning with salt if needed. Simmer for another 5 minutes. Remove lemongrass, kaffir lime leaves, and galangal or ginger slices before serving.

2. Prepare the Ramen and Toppings:

- Cook ramen noodles according to package instructions. Drain and set aside.
- In a separate pan, heat vegetable oil over medium heat. Add onion and bell pepper slices, sauté until softened, about 3-4 minutes.
- Add sliced mushrooms and tofu cubes, cook for another 3-4 minutes until mushrooms are tender.
- Add baby spinach and cook briefly until wilted.

3. Assemble Tom Yum Ramen:

- Divide cooked ramen noodles among serving bowls.
- Ladle the hot Tom Yum broth over the noodles.
- Top with sautéed vegetables and tofu mixture.
- Arrange soft-boiled egg halves on top.

4. Garnish and Serve:

- Garnish each bowl with chopped fresh cilantro and serve with lime wedges on the side.
- Serve hot and enjoy the aromatic and spicy flavors of Tom Yum Ramen!

Notes:

- **Spice Level:** Adjust the spiciness of the ramen by varying the amount of Thai bird's eye chilies and Thai chili paste (Nam Prik Pao) according to your preference.
- **Vegetarian/Vegan Option:** Use vegetable broth and omit the fish sauce or substitute with soy sauce for a vegetarian or vegan version.
- **Toppings:** Customize your Tom Yum Ramen with additional toppings such as bean sprouts, bamboo shoots, or Thai basil for added texture and flavor.
- **Make Ahead:** The broth can be prepared ahead of time and stored in the refrigerator for up to 3 days. Reheat gently before serving over freshly cooked noodles and toppings.

Enjoy the vibrant and spicy flavors of homemade Tom Yum Ramen, perfect for a unique and satisfying meal!

Mapo Tofu Ramen

Ingredients:

For the Mapo Tofu Sauce:

- 200g ground pork (or substitute with ground chicken or beef)
- 2 tablespoons vegetable oil
- 2 cloves garlic, minced
- 1-inch piece ginger, grated
- 2 tablespoons doubanjiang (spicy fermented bean paste)
- 1 tablespoon chili bean paste (Toban Djan)
- 1 tablespoon soy sauce
- 1 tablespoon sake or rice wine
- 1 tablespoon sugar
- 1 cup chicken or vegetable broth
- 1 block (about 300g) silken tofu, cut into cubes
- 1 tablespoon cornstarch mixed with 2 tablespoons water (optional, for thickening)

For the Ramen:

- 300g ramen noodles (fresh or dried)
- 4 cups chicken or vegetable broth
- 2 cups water
- 2 tablespoons soy sauce
- 1 tablespoon sesame oil
- Salt, to taste

For Toppings (Optional):

- Soft-boiled eggs, halved
- Sliced green onions (scallions)
- Nori (seaweed), shredded
- Sesame seeds

Instructions:

1. Prepare the Mapo Tofu Sauce:

- Heat vegetable oil in a large skillet or wok over medium-high heat. Add minced garlic and grated ginger, sauté for 1-2 minutes until fragrant.
- Add ground pork (or substitute) and cook until browned and cooked through.
- Stir in doubanjiang, chili bean paste (Toban Djan), soy sauce, sake or rice wine, and sugar. Cook for another 1-2 minutes to combine flavors.

- Pour in chicken or vegetable broth and bring to a simmer. Add tofu cubes gently and simmer for 5-7 minutes.
- If you prefer a thicker sauce, stir in cornstarch mixture and simmer until sauce thickens slightly. Remove from heat and set aside.

2. Prepare the Ramen:

- Cook ramen noodles according to package instructions. Drain and set aside.
- In a separate pot, combine chicken or vegetable broth and water. Bring to a boil over medium-high heat.
- Stir in soy sauce and sesame oil. Taste and adjust seasoning with salt if needed.

3. Assemble Mapo Tofu Ramen:

- Divide cooked ramen noodles among serving bowls.
- Ladle the hot broth over the noodles.
- Spoon a generous amount of Mapo Tofu sauce with tofu cubes over the noodles and broth.

4. Garnish and Serve:

- Garnish each bowl with soft-boiled egg halves, sliced green onions (scallions), shredded nori (seaweed), and sesame seeds.
- Serve hot and enjoy the bold and spicy flavors of Mapo Tofu Ramen!

Notes:

- **Spice Level:** Adjust the spiciness of the Mapo Tofu sauce by varying the amount of doubanjiang and chili bean paste according to your preference.
- **Protein Variation:** You can use ground chicken or beef instead of pork, or skip the meat altogether for a vegetarian version.
- **Toppings:** Customize your Mapo Tofu Ramen with additional toppings such as bamboo shoots, bean sprouts, or blanched spinach for added texture and flavor.
- **Make Ahead:** The Mapo Tofu sauce can be prepared ahead of time and stored in the refrigerator for up to 3 days. Reheat gently before serving over freshly cooked noodles and broth.

Enjoy the flavorful and satisfying Mapo Tofu Ramen, combining the best of both worlds in one delicious bowl!

Jjajang Ramen (Black Bean Noodles)

Ingredients:

For the Black Bean Sauce (Jjajang):

- 200g pork belly or shoulder, thinly sliced
- 2 tablespoons vegetable oil
- 1 onion, finely diced
- 1 zucchini, diced
- 1 small potato, diced
- 1/2 cup black bean paste (Jjajang paste)
- 1 tablespoon soy sauce
- 1 tablespoon oyster sauce
- 1 tablespoon sugar
- 1 cup chicken or vegetable broth
- 2 tablespoons cornstarch mixed with 3 tablespoons water (optional, for thickening)

For the Ramen:

- 300g ramen noodles (fresh or dried)
- 4 cups water
- 2 cups chicken or vegetable broth
- 2 tablespoons soy sauce
- 1 tablespoon sesame oil
- Soft-boiled eggs, halved (optional)
- Sliced cucumber or radish (optional, for garnish)
- Sliced green onions (scallions), for garnish

Instructions:

1. Prepare the Black Bean Sauce (Jjajang):

- Heat vegetable oil in a large skillet or wok over medium-high heat. Add pork slices and cook until browned and cooked through.
- Add diced onion, zucchini, and potato to the skillet. Sauté for 3-4 minutes until vegetables start to soften.
- Stir in black bean paste (Jjajang paste), soy sauce, oyster sauce, and sugar. Cook for 2-3 minutes until fragrant.
- Pour in chicken or vegetable broth and bring to a simmer. Reduce heat to low and simmer for 10-15 minutes, stirring occasionally.
- If you prefer a thicker sauce, stir in cornstarch mixture and simmer until sauce thickens. Remove from heat and set aside.

2. Prepare the Ramen:

- Cook ramen noodles according to package instructions. Drain and set aside.
- In a separate pot, bring water and chicken or vegetable broth to a boil over medium-high heat.
- Stir in soy sauce and sesame oil. Taste and adjust seasoning with salt if needed.

3. Assemble Jjajang Ramen:

- Divide cooked ramen noodles among serving bowls.
- Ladle the hot broth over the noodles.
- Spoon a generous amount of Jjajang sauce with pork and vegetables over the noodles and broth.

4. Garnish and Serve:

- Garnish each bowl with soft-boiled egg halves (if using), sliced cucumber or radish (if using), and sliced green onions (scallions).
- Serve hot and enjoy the savory and satisfying flavors of Jjajang Ramen!

Notes:

- **Black Bean Paste (Jjajang Paste):** You can find Jjajang paste in Korean or Asian grocery stores. It's a fermented black bean paste that gives the dish its signature flavor.
- **Vegetarian/Vegan Option:** Omit the pork and use tofu or mushrooms as a substitute for a vegetarian or vegan version. Adjust seasoning accordingly.
- **Toppings:** Customize your Jjajang Ramen with additional toppings such as kimchi, pickled radish, or stir-fried vegetables for added texture and flavor.
- **Make Ahead:** The Jjajang sauce can be prepared ahead of time and stored in the refrigerator for up to 3 days. Reheat gently before serving over freshly cooked noodles and broth.

Enjoy making and savoring this delicious Korean-Chinese fusion dish of Jjajang Ramen!

Tomato Ramen

Ingredients:

For the Broth:

- 4 cups chicken or vegetable broth
- 2 cups water
- 2 tomatoes, chopped
- 1 onion, chopped
- 2 cloves garlic, minced
- 1 tablespoon tomato paste
- 1 tablespoon soy sauce
- 1 tablespoon miso paste
- 1 tablespoon sesame oil
- Salt and pepper, to taste

For the Ramen:

- 300g ramen noodles (fresh or dried)
- 1 tablespoon vegetable oil
- 1 bell pepper, thinly sliced
- 1 cup mushrooms (shiitake or button), sliced
- 2 cups baby spinach
- 2 soft-boiled eggs, halved (optional)
- Fresh basil leaves, chopped, for garnish
- Grated Parmesan cheese, for garnish (optional)

Instructions:

1. Prepare the Broth:

- In a large pot, combine chicken or vegetable broth and water. Bring to a boil over medium-high heat.
- Add chopped tomatoes, onion, and minced garlic to the pot. Simmer for 10-15 minutes until vegetables are tender.
- Stir in tomato paste, soy sauce, miso paste, and sesame oil. Simmer for another 5 minutes to blend flavors.
- Season with salt and pepper to taste. Adjust seasoning as needed.

2. Prepare the Ramen and Toppings:

- Cook ramen noodles according to package instructions. Drain and set aside.
- In a separate pan, heat vegetable oil over medium heat. Add sliced bell pepper and mushrooms. Sauté until vegetables are tender, about 4-5 minutes.

- Add baby spinach to the pan and cook briefly until wilted.

3. Assemble Tomato Ramen:

- Divide cooked ramen noodles among serving bowls.
- Ladle the hot tomato broth over the noodles.
- Top with sautéed vegetables.
- If using, place soft-boiled egg halves on top of the ramen bowls.

4. Garnish and Serve:

- Garnish each bowl with chopped fresh basil leaves and grated Parmesan cheese (if using).
- Serve hot and enjoy the comforting and flavorful Tomato Ramen!

Notes:

- **Tomato Paste:** You can use canned tomato paste or fresh tomato puree for a richer tomato flavor.
- **Vegetarian/Vegan Option:** Use vegetable broth and omit the eggs and Parmesan cheese for a vegetarian or vegan version.
- **Toppings:** Customize your Tomato Ramen with additional toppings such as grilled chicken slices, cherry tomatoes, or a drizzle of balsamic glaze for added depth.
- **Make Ahead:** The tomato broth can be prepared ahead of time and stored in the refrigerator for up to 3 days. Reheat gently before serving over freshly cooked noodles and toppings.

Enjoy the unique blend of Japanese and Italian flavors in this comforting Tomato Ramen dish!

Fried Chicken Ramen

Ingredients:

For the Fried Chicken:

- 2 boneless, skinless chicken breasts
- Salt and pepper, to taste
- 1 cup all-purpose flour
- 2 eggs, beaten
- 1 cup panko breadcrumbs
- Vegetable oil, for frying

For the Ramen:

- 300g ramen noodles (fresh or dried)
- 4 cups chicken broth
- 2 cups water
- 2 tablespoons soy sauce
- 1 tablespoon sesame oil

For Toppings:

- Soft-boiled eggs, halved
- Sliced green onions (scallions)
- Nori (seaweed), shredded
- Sesame seeds
- Optional: Corn kernels, bamboo shoots, spinach

Instructions:

1. Prepare the Fried Chicken:

- Cut chicken breasts into thin strips or bite-sized pieces. Season with salt and pepper.
- Set up a breading station: Place flour in one shallow bowl, beaten eggs in another bowl, and panko breadcrumbs in a third bowl.
- Dredge each piece of chicken in flour, dip into beaten eggs, then coat evenly with panko breadcrumbs, pressing gently to adhere.
- Heat vegetable oil in a large skillet or deep fryer over medium-high heat. Fry chicken pieces in batches until golden brown and cooked through, about 3-4 minutes per side. Transfer to a plate lined with paper towels to drain excess oil.

2. Prepare the Ramen:

- Cook ramen noodles according to package instructions. Drain and set aside.
- In a separate pot, bring chicken broth and water to a boil over medium-high heat.

- Stir in soy sauce and sesame oil. Taste and adjust seasoning with salt if needed.

3. Assemble Fried Chicken Ramen:

- Divide cooked ramen noodles among serving bowls.
- Ladle the hot broth over the noodles.
- Top with fried chicken pieces.

4. Garnish and Serve:

- Arrange soft-boiled egg halves, sliced green onions (scallions), shredded nori (seaweed), and sesame seeds on top of each bowl.
- Add any additional toppings such as corn kernels, bamboo shoots, or spinach if desired.
- Serve hot and enjoy the delicious and comforting Fried Chicken Ramen!

Notes:

- **Frying Tips:** Ensure the oil is hot enough (around 350°F/175°C) before frying the chicken to achieve crispy results. Fry in batches to avoid overcrowding the pan.
- **Variations:** Customize your Fried Chicken Ramen by adding different vegetables or adjusting the broth seasoning according to your taste preferences.
- **Make Ahead:** You can prepare the fried chicken ahead of time and reheat in the oven to maintain crispiness before serving with freshly cooked ramen and hot broth.

Enjoy this hearty and satisfying Fried Chicken Ramen, perfect for a comforting meal any day of the week!

Tempura Ramen

Ingredients:

For the Tempura:

- Assorted vegetables (such as sweet potato, zucchini, bell peppers, and mushrooms), thinly sliced
- 8 large shrimp, peeled and deveined
- 1 cup all-purpose flour
- 1/2 cup cornstarch
- 1 teaspoon baking powder
- 1 cup ice-cold water
- Vegetable oil, for frying
- Salt, to taste

For the Ramen:

- 300g ramen noodles (fresh or dried)
- 4 cups chicken or vegetable broth
- 2 cups water
- 2 tablespoons soy sauce
- 1 tablespoon mirin (Japanese sweet rice wine)
- 1 tablespoon sesame oil
- Salt, to taste

For Toppings:

- Soft-boiled eggs, halved
- Sliced green onions (scallions)
- Nori (seaweed), shredded
- Optional: Bamboo shoots, bean sprouts, sliced mushrooms

Instructions:

1. Prepare the Tempura:

- In a large bowl, combine all-purpose flour, cornstarch, baking powder, and a pinch of salt.
- Gradually add ice-cold water to the dry ingredients, whisking gently until just combined. The batter should be slightly lumpy.
- Heat vegetable oil in a deep fryer or large pot to 350°F (175°C).
- Dip sliced vegetables and shrimp into the tempura batter, shaking off any excess, and carefully lower them into the hot oil. Fry in batches until golden brown and crispy, about 2-3 minutes per side. Transfer to a plate lined with paper towels to drain excess oil.

2. Prepare the Ramen:

- Cook ramen noodles according to package instructions. Drain and set aside.
- In a separate pot, bring chicken or vegetable broth and water to a boil over medium-high heat.
- Stir in soy sauce, mirin, and sesame oil. Taste and adjust seasoning with salt if needed.

3. Assemble Tempura Ramen:

- Divide cooked ramen noodles among serving bowls.
- Ladle the hot broth over the noodles.
- Arrange tempura vegetables and shrimp on top of the ramen bowls.

4. Garnish and Serve:

- Garnish each bowl with soft-boiled egg halves, sliced green onions (scallions), shredded nori (seaweed), and any additional toppings like bamboo shoots or bean sprouts.
- Serve hot and enjoy the crispy, flavorful Tempura Ramen!

Notes:

- **Tempura Tips:** Fry the tempura batches just before serving to maintain their crispiness. You can also use your favorite vegetables or seafood for the tempura.
- **Broth Variation:** Feel free to customize the broth by adding dashi stock or miso paste for added depth of flavor.
- **Make Ahead:** Prepare the tempura batter and vegetables ahead of time, but fry them just before serving to ensure they remain crispy.

Enjoy this delicious fusion of tempura and ramen with the flavors and textures that complement each other perfectly in Tempura Ramen!

Uni (Sea Urchin) Ramen

Ingredients:

For the Broth:

- 4 cups dashi stock (homemade or store-bought)
- 2 cups water
- 1 cup seafood broth (optional, for extra depth)
- 1 tablespoon soy sauce
- 1 tablespoon mirin (Japanese sweet rice wine)
- Salt, to taste

For the Ramen:

- 300g ramen noodles (fresh or dried)
- 4-6 pieces uni (sea urchin), depending on size and preference
- 1 tablespoon unsalted butter
- 1 tablespoon soy sauce
- 1 tablespoon mirin
- 1 teaspoon sesame oil

For Toppings:

- Nori (seaweed), thinly sliced
- Green onions (scallions), thinly sliced
- Soft-boiled eggs, halved
- Optional: Steamed vegetables (like spinach or bean sprouts), sliced mushrooms

Instructions:

1. Prepare the Broth:

- In a large pot, combine dashi stock, water, and seafood broth (if using). Bring to a gentle simmer over medium heat.
- Stir in soy sauce, mirin, and salt to taste. Adjust seasoning as needed. Keep the broth warm over low heat while preparing the rest of the dish.

2. Prepare the Uni Mixture:

- In a small bowl, combine uni (sea urchin) with unsalted butter, soy sauce, mirin, and sesame oil. Mash and mix until well combined. Set aside.

3. Prepare the Ramen:

- Cook ramen noodles according to package instructions. Drain and set aside.

- Divide the warm broth among serving bowls.
- Add a spoonful of the uni mixture to each bowl of hot broth and gently stir to incorporate.
- Add cooked ramen noodles to each bowl, arranging them evenly.

4. Garnish and Serve:

- Garnish each bowl with thinly sliced nori (seaweed), green onions (scallions), and soft-boiled egg halves.
- Optional: Add steamed vegetables or sliced mushrooms as additional toppings for extra texture and flavor.
- Serve hot and enjoy the luxurious and briny flavors of Uni Ramen!

Notes:

- **Uni (Sea Urchin):** Choose fresh uni from a reputable source. The flavor can vary, so adjust the amount used based on personal preference.
- **Broth Variation:** For a creamier broth, you can add a splash of heavy cream or coconut milk to the broth before serving.
- **Make Ahead:** Prepare the broth and uni mixture ahead of time, but assemble and heat just before serving to maintain the best texture and flavor.

Uni Ramen offers a unique and indulgent experience, blending the delicate sweetness of sea urchin with the comforting warmth of ramen noodles. Enjoy this special dish for a luxurious meal at home!

Gyukotsu Ramen (Beef Bone Ramen)

Ingredients:

For the Broth:

- 3-4 lbs beef bones (marrow bones and knuckle bones)
- 1 onion, halved
- 2 carrots, chopped
- 3 garlic cloves, smashed
- 2-inch piece of ginger, sliced
- 1 leek, chopped
- 1 tablespoon vegetable oil
- 10 cups water
- 1 cup soy sauce
- 1/2 cup mirin (Japanese sweet rice wine)
- 2 tablespoons sake (Japanese rice wine)
- Salt, to taste

For the Ramen:

- 300g ramen noodles (fresh or dried)
- 4 soft-boiled eggs, halved
- Sliced green onions (scallions)
- Nori (seaweed), shredded
- Bamboo shoots, sliced (optional)
- Bean sprouts (optional)
- Black garlic oil or sesame oil (optional, for drizzling)

Instructions:

1. Prepare the Broth:

- Preheat your oven to 400°F (200°C). Place beef bones on a baking sheet and roast in the oven for 30-40 minutes until browned.
- In a large pot, heat vegetable oil over medium-high heat. Add onion, carrots, garlic, ginger, and leek. Sauté for 5-7 minutes until vegetables are lightly browned.
- Add roasted beef bones to the pot. Pour in water, soy sauce, mirin, and sake. Bring to a boil over high heat.
- Reduce heat to low and simmer, uncovered, for 8-10 hours, skimming off any foam and fat that rises to the surface. The longer you simmer, the richer the broth will become.
- Strain the broth through a fine-mesh sieve or cheesecloth into a clean pot. Discard solids. Season with salt to taste.

2. Prepare the Ramen:

- Cook ramen noodles according to package instructions. Drain and set aside.
- Reheat the beef bone broth until hot.

3. Assemble Gyukotsu Ramen:

- Divide cooked ramen noodles among serving bowls.
- Ladle the hot beef bone broth over the noodles, filling each bowl generously.
- Top each bowl with soft-boiled egg halves, sliced green onions (scallions), shredded nori (seaweed), and any additional toppings like bamboo shoots or bean sprouts.
- Optional: Drizzle with black garlic oil or sesame oil for added flavor.

4. Garnish and Serve:

- Serve hot and enjoy the rich and flavorful Gyukotsu Ramen!

Notes:

- **Beef Bones:** Look for beef bones with marrow and knuckle bones for the richest broth. You can also include oxtail for additional flavor.
- **Simmering Time:** The key to Gyukotsu Ramen is the long simmering time, which extracts maximum flavor from the bones. Plan ahead as this can be a time-consuming process.
- **Toppings:** Customize your Gyukotsu Ramen with your favorite toppings such as corn kernels, mushrooms, or a sprinkle of togarashi (Japanese chili pepper) for a spicy kick.
- **Make Ahead:** Gyukotsu Ramen broth freezes well. Prepare a large batch and freeze in portions for quick and easy ramen meals later.

Enjoy creating this hearty and flavorful Gyukotsu Ramen at home, perfect for a comforting and satisfying meal!

Chicken Shio Ramen

Ingredients:

For the Chicken Broth:

- 2 lbs chicken bones (backs, wings, or a whole chicken carcass)
- 8 cups water
- 1 onion, quartered
- 2 carrots, chopped
- 2 celery stalks, chopped
- 3 garlic cloves, smashed
- 2-inch piece of ginger, sliced
- 2 green onions (scallions), chopped
- 2 tablespoons soy sauce
- 1 tablespoon salt (adjust to taste)
- 1 tablespoon mirin (Japanese sweet rice wine)
- 1 tablespoon sesame oil

For the Ramen:

- 300g ramen noodles (fresh or dried)
- 4 soft-boiled eggs, halved
- Sliced bamboo shoots (menma)
- Sliced green onions (scallions)
- Nori (seaweed), shredded
- Optional: Corn kernels, spinach, bean sprouts

Instructions:

1. Prepare the Chicken Broth:

- In a large pot, combine chicken bones, water, onion, carrots, celery, garlic, ginger, and green onions.
- Bring to a boil over high heat. Skim off any foam that rises to the surface.
- Reduce heat to low and simmer, uncovered, for 2-3 hours. The longer you simmer, the richer the broth will become.
- Strain the broth through a fine-mesh sieve or cheesecloth into a clean pot. Discard solids.
- Stir in soy sauce, salt, mirin, and sesame oil. Adjust seasoning to taste.

2. Prepare the Ramen:

- Cook ramen noodles according to package instructions. Drain and set aside.
- Reheat the chicken broth until hot.

3. Assemble Chicken Shio Ramen:

- Divide cooked ramen noodles among serving bowls.
- Ladle the hot chicken broth over the noodles, filling each bowl generously.
- Top each bowl with soft-boiled egg halves, sliced bamboo shoots (menma), sliced green onions (scallions), and shredded nori (seaweed).
- Optional: Add other toppings such as corn kernels, spinach, or bean sprouts for added texture and flavor.

4. Garnish and Serve:

- Serve hot and enjoy the delicate and savory Chicken Shio Ramen!

Notes:

- **Chicken Bones:** You can use a combination of chicken bones such as backs, wings, or a whole chicken carcass for the broth. This will provide a rich chicken flavor.
- **Toppings:** Customize your Chicken Shio Ramen with your favorite toppings. Traditional toppings include soft-boiled eggs, bamboo shoots, green onions, and nori.
- **Make Ahead:** The broth can be prepared ahead of time and stored in the refrigerator for up to 3 days or frozen for longer storage. Reheat gently before serving with freshly cooked ramen noodles.

Enjoy making and savoring this comforting and flavorful Chicken Shio Ramen at home!

Spicy Shrimp Ramen

Ingredients:

For the Broth:

- 4 cups chicken or seafood broth
- 2 cups water
- 2 tablespoons soy sauce
- 2 tablespoons mirin (Japanese sweet rice wine)
- 2 tablespoons sesame oil
- 2 tablespoons gochujang (Korean red chili paste), or to taste
- 1 tablespoon miso paste
- 3 cloves garlic, minced
- 1-inch piece of ginger, grated
- Salt, to taste

For the Ramen:

- 300g ramen noodles (fresh or dried)
- 1 lb shrimp, peeled and deveined
- 2 tablespoons vegetable oil
- Salt and pepper, to taste
- 2 soft-boiled eggs, halved (optional)
- Sliced green onions (scallions)
- Nori (seaweed), shredded
- Bean sprouts (optional)
- Lime wedges, for serving

Instructions:

1. Prepare the Broth:

- In a large pot, combine chicken or seafood broth, water, soy sauce, mirin, sesame oil, gochujang, miso paste, garlic, and ginger.
- Bring the broth to a boil over medium-high heat, then reduce heat and simmer for 10-15 minutes to allow flavors to meld together. Taste and adjust seasoning with salt if needed.

2. Prepare the Shrimp:

- Heat vegetable oil in a large skillet over medium-high heat.
- Season shrimp with salt and pepper. Cook shrimp in the skillet for 2-3 minutes per side until pink and cooked through. Remove from heat and set aside.

3. Prepare the Ramen Noodles:

- Cook ramen noodles according to package instructions. Drain and set aside.

4. Assemble Spicy Shrimp Ramen:

- Divide cooked ramen noodles among serving bowls.
- Ladle the hot spicy broth over the noodles, ensuring each bowl gets a good amount of broth.
- Arrange cooked shrimp on top of each bowl of ramen.

5. Garnish and Serve:

- Top each bowl with soft-boiled egg halves (if using), sliced green onions (scallions), shredded nori (seaweed), and bean sprouts.
- Serve hot with lime wedges on the side for squeezing over the ramen to add a fresh citrusy flavor.

Notes:

- **Spice Level:** Adjust the amount of gochujang according to your spice preference. You can start with less and add more gradually to achieve the desired level of spiciness.
- **Toppings:** Feel free to customize your Spicy Shrimp Ramen with additional toppings such as corn kernels, sliced mushrooms, or spinach.
- **Make Ahead:** The broth can be made ahead of time and stored in the refrigerator for up to 3 days. Reheat gently before serving with freshly cooked ramen noodles and shrimp.

Enjoy the bold and spicy flavors of this homemade Spicy Shrimp Ramen, perfect for warming up on chilly days.

Duck Shoyu Ramen

Ingredients:

For the Broth:

- 2 duck legs or 1 whole duck breast
- 8 cups chicken broth
- 2 cups water
- 1 onion, halved
- 2 carrots, chopped
- 2 celery stalks, chopped
- 3 garlic cloves, smashed
- 2-inch piece of ginger, sliced
- 2 green onions (scallions), chopped
- 1/2 cup soy sauce
- 2 tablespoons mirin (Japanese sweet rice wine)
- 1 tablespoon sesame oil
- Salt and pepper, to taste

For the Ramen:

- 300g ramen noodles (fresh or dried)
- 4 soft-boiled eggs, halved
- Sliced bamboo shoots (menma)
- Sliced green onions (scallions)
- Nori (seaweed), shredded
- Optional: Corn kernels, spinach, bean sprouts

Instructions:

1. Prepare the Duck Broth:

- If using duck legs, sear them in a large pot over medium-high heat until browned on both sides. If using duck breast, skip this step.
- Add chicken broth, water, onion, carrots, celery, garlic, ginger, and green onions to the pot.
- Bring to a boil over high heat. Skim off any foam that rises to the surface.
- Reduce heat to low and simmer, partially covered, for 1.5 to 2 hours until the duck is tender and cooked through.
- Remove the duck legs or breast from the broth. Allow them to cool slightly, then shred the meat using two forks. Set aside.
- Strain the broth through a fine-mesh sieve or cheesecloth into a clean pot. Discard solids.
- Stir in soy sauce, mirin, sesame oil, salt, and pepper. Adjust seasoning to taste.

2. Prepare the Ramen:

- Cook ramen noodles according to package instructions. Drain and set aside.

3. Assemble Duck Shoyu Ramen:

- Divide cooked ramen noodles among serving bowls.
- Ladle the hot duck broth over the noodles, ensuring each bowl gets a generous amount of broth.
- Top each bowl with shredded duck meat, soft-boiled egg halves, sliced bamboo shoots (menma), sliced green onions (scallions), and shredded nori (seaweed).
- Optional: Add other toppings such as corn kernels, spinach, or bean sprouts for added texture and flavor.

4. Garnish and Serve:

- Serve hot and enjoy the rich and savory Duck Shoyu Ramen!

Notes:

- **Duck Meat:** Duck legs are preferred for this recipe as they contribute to a richer broth. You can also use a whole duck breast for a quicker cooking time.
- **Make Ahead:** The broth can be prepared ahead of time and stored in the refrigerator for up to 3 days or frozen for longer storage. Reheat gently before serving with freshly cooked ramen noodles and toppings.
- **Variation:** For an extra depth of flavor, you can roast the duck legs or breast before adding them to the broth.

Enjoy making this Duck Shoyu Ramen at home, bringing together the comforting flavors of duck with a classic soy sauce broth for a satisfying meal!

Spicy Crab Ramen

Ingredients:

For the Spicy Crab Broth:

- 4 cups chicken or seafood broth
- 2 cups water
- 2 tablespoons soy sauce
- 2 tablespoons mirin (Japanese sweet rice wine)
- 2 tablespoons gochujang (Korean red chili paste), or to taste
- 1 tablespoon sesame oil
- 1 tablespoon miso paste
- 3 cloves garlic, minced
- 1-inch piece of ginger, grated
- 1 lb crab legs or lump crab meat
- Salt, to taste

For the Ramen:

- 300g ramen noodles (fresh or dried)
- 1 lb crab legs or lump crab meat, cooked and picked
- 2 soft-boiled eggs, halved
- Sliced green onions (scallions)
- Nori (seaweed), shredded
- Bean sprouts (optional)
- Lime wedges, for serving

Instructions:

1. Prepare the Spicy Crab Broth:

- In a large pot, combine chicken or seafood broth, water, soy sauce, mirin, gochujang, sesame oil, miso paste, garlic, and ginger.
- Bring the broth to a boil over medium-high heat. Reduce heat and simmer for 10-15 minutes to allow flavors to meld together.
- Add crab legs or lump crab meat to the broth. Simmer for an additional 5-7 minutes until the crab is heated through and flavors are infused. Remove crab legs from the broth and set aside.
- Taste the broth and adjust seasoning with salt if needed.

2. Prepare the Ramen Noodles:

- Cook ramen noodles according to package instructions. Drain and set aside.

3. Assemble Spicy Crab Ramen:

- Divide cooked ramen noodles among serving bowls.
- Ladle the hot spicy crab broth over the noodles, ensuring each bowl gets a good amount of broth.
- Top each bowl with picked crab meat, soft-boiled egg halves, sliced green onions (scallions), shredded nori (seaweed), and bean sprouts (if using).
- Serve hot with lime wedges on the side for squeezing over the ramen to add a fresh citrusy flavor.

Notes:

- **Crab Meat:** Use fresh crab legs or lump crab meat for the best flavor. You can also use a combination of both if desired.
- **Spice Level:** Adjust the amount of gochujang according to your spice preference. Start with less and add more gradually to achieve the desired level of spiciness.
- **Toppings:** Customize your Spicy Crab Ramen with additional toppings such as corn kernels, sliced mushrooms, or spinach.
- **Make Ahead:** The broth can be made ahead of time and stored in the refrigerator for up to 3 days. Reheat gently before serving with freshly cooked ramen noodles and crab meat.

Enjoy the delicious and spicy flavors of homemade Spicy Crab Ramen, perfect for a comforting and satisfying meal!

Get smarter responses, upload files and images, and

Mushroom Ramen

Ingredients:

For the Broth:

- 8 cups vegetable broth (or mushroom broth for even more mushroom flavor)
- 2 cups water
- 4 cloves garlic, minced
- 2-inch piece of ginger, sliced
- 1 onion, sliced
- 1 leek, chopped
- 1 carrot, chopped
- 1 celery stalk, chopped
- 1 tablespoon soy sauce
- 1 tablespoon miso paste
- 1 tablespoon mirin (Japanese sweet rice wine)
- Salt and pepper, to taste

For the Ramen:

- 300g ramen noodles (fresh or dried)
- 300g mixed mushrooms (shiitake, oyster, enoki, etc.), sliced
- 2 tablespoons vegetable oil
- 2 soft-boiled eggs, halved (optional)
- Sliced green onions (scallions)
- Nori (seaweed), shredded
- Bean sprouts (optional)
- Sesame seeds, for garnish

Instructions:

1. Prepare the Mushroom Broth:

- In a large pot, combine vegetable broth, water, garlic, ginger, onion, leek, carrot, and celery.
- Bring to a boil over high heat. Reduce heat to low and simmer, partially covered, for 30-40 minutes to allow flavors to develop.
- Stir in soy sauce, miso paste, and mirin. Season with salt and pepper to taste. Simmer for an additional 10 minutes. Remove from heat and keep warm.

2. Prepare the Mushrooms:

- In a separate skillet, heat vegetable oil over medium-high heat.

- Add mixed mushrooms and sauté for 5-7 minutes until mushrooms are tender and lightly browned. Set aside.

3. Prepare the Ramen Noodles:

- Cook ramen noodles according to package instructions. Drain and set aside.

4. Assemble Mushroom Ramen:

- Divide cooked ramen noodles among serving bowls.
- Ladle the hot mushroom broth over the noodles, ensuring each bowl gets a generous amount of broth.
- Top each bowl with sautéed mushrooms, soft-boiled egg halves (if using), sliced green onions (scallions), shredded nori (seaweed), and bean sprouts (if using).
- Sprinkle with sesame seeds for garnish.

5. Garnish and Serve:

- Serve hot and enjoy the comforting and flavorful Mushroom Ramen!

Notes:

- **Variety of Mushrooms:** Use a combination of different mushrooms for depth of flavor. Shiitake, oyster mushrooms, enoki, and cremini mushrooms work well.
- **Make Ahead:** The broth can be made ahead of time and stored in the refrigerator for up to 3 days. Reheat gently before serving with freshly cooked ramen noodles and toppings.
- **Toppings:** Customize your Mushroom Ramen with additional toppings such as bamboo shoots, corn kernels, or spinach.

This Mushroom Ramen recipe offers a satisfying and vegetarian-friendly alternative to traditional ramen, highlighting the earthy and savory flavors of mushrooms in a comforting bowl of noodles.

Yuzu Ramen

Ingredients:

For the Broth:

- 6 cups chicken or vegetable broth
- 2 cups water
- 3 cloves garlic, minced
- 2-inch piece of ginger, sliced
- 1 onion, sliced
- 2 tablespoons soy sauce
- 1 tablespoon mirin (Japanese sweet rice wine)
- 1 tablespoon sesame oil
- Juice and zest of 1-2 yuzu fruits (adjust to taste)
- Salt and pepper, to taste

For the Ramen:

- 300g ramen noodles (fresh or dried)
- 300g thinly sliced pork belly or chicken breast (optional)
- 2 soft-boiled eggs, halved
- Sliced green onions (scallions)
- Nori (seaweed), shredded
- Bean sprouts (optional)
- Yuzu slices, for garnish (optional)

Instructions:

1. Prepare the Broth:

- In a large pot, combine chicken or vegetable broth, water, garlic, ginger, and onion.
- Bring to a boil over high heat. Reduce heat to low and simmer, partially covered, for 30 minutes to allow flavors to meld together.
- Stir in soy sauce, mirin, sesame oil, and yuzu juice and zest. Season with salt and pepper to taste. Simmer for an additional 10 minutes. Remove from heat and keep warm.

2. Prepare the Ramen Noodles:

- Cook ramen noodles according to package instructions. Drain and set aside.

3. Optional: Prepare the Protein (Pork Belly or Chicken):

- If using pork belly or chicken, thinly slice and cook in a separate skillet over medium-high heat until cooked through and lightly browned. Set aside.

4. Assemble Yuzu Ramen:

- Divide cooked ramen noodles among serving bowls.
- Ladle the hot yuzu broth over the noodles, ensuring each bowl gets a generous amount of broth.
- Top each bowl with cooked pork belly or chicken (if using), soft-boiled egg halves, sliced green onions (scallions), shredded nori (seaweed), and bean sprouts (if using).
- Garnish with yuzu slices for an extra burst of citrus flavor (optional).

5. Garnish and Serve:

- Serve hot and enjoy the refreshing and citrusy flavors of Yuzu Ramen!

Notes:

- **Yuzu Juice and Zest:** Yuzu can vary in flavor intensity, so adjust the amount of juice and zest based on your preference and the fruit's flavor profile.
- **Make Ahead:** The broth can be made ahead of time and stored in the refrigerator for up to 3 days. Reheat gently before serving with freshly cooked ramen noodles and toppings.
- **Toppings:** Customize your Yuzu Ramen with additional toppings such as bamboo shoots, corn kernels, or spinach.

Enjoy this unique and flavorful Yuzu Ramen recipe, perfect for a bright and satisfying meal with a citrusy twist!

www.ingramcontent.com/pod-product-compliance
Lightning Source LLC
LaVergne TN
LVHW081557060526
838201LV00054B/1931